CW00673996

LLOYDS BANK

Clearing Department of Cox & Co, Charing Cross, London, about 1920.

LLOYDS BANK

A Pictorial History with Text and Staff Anecdotes

250th Anniversary Limited Edition

A Personal View
Written and Researched
by
Richard Hart

Richard Hart

Signed by the author

67

First Published 1989
Revised Edition 2015
for the 250th Anniversary

ISBN: 978-0-9511698-7-2

Printed by Berforts Information Press Ltd, Stevenage

Published by Farnon Books
Leighton Buzzard

Foreword

Over the years, many authors have drawn material and inspiration from the assembled records of Lloyds Bank. The archive service is glad to offer information and facilities to bona fide historians from within and without the Bank. Richard Hart, the latest in this line of researchers, has been particularly enthusiastic in his enquiries, which have embraced almost every aspect of the Bank's growth and business.

While this book is not an official publication of Lloyds Bank, and the findings and facts, as they are presented, are the responsibility of the author, I am pleased to commend it to present and former members of staff who will, I know, find a wealth of detail and illustrations to interest them and a fund of anecdotes to make mellow a rainy weekend.

John Booker, BA, MLitt, DPhil, FRHistS
Archivist and Curator
Lloyds Bank Plc

This book is dedicated to all the men and women
who have helped make Lloyds Bank such a success over the years

Contents

Acknowledgements

The author wishes to thank everyone who has helped in his research or loaned pictures. In particular his gratitude goes to his wife Jackie without whose support this work would have never been completed. Space does not permit mention of everybody who assisted in the original publication. Having thanked those who have made substantial contributions to the book the author wishes to emphasize that any errors or omissions are his own.

Grateful thanks go to Dr John Booker for honouring this book with a Foreword. He contributed many suggestions for improving or adding to the content. In addition his staff namely Paula Smith, Alan Burville and Sally Coey have been very helpful and friendly.

Other members of staff who have helped include: Len Bickley, Elaine Crew, Brian Johnson, Fay Moffet, E.W.Peck, Glenys Phillips, Tony Prior, John and Christine Roberts. Alex Richmond-Scott, Stella Snell, Robert Surrey, Stephen Whittam and Keith Wigmore.

Former members of staff and their relatives who have contributed include: Drusilla Armitage, Doreen Beaton, Margaret Bickel, Mrs E.G. Brookes, Doreen Budgett, R.W. Currell, S. Gelder, A.E. Harding, R.F.S. Kipling, Stella Lowen, Janet Pusey, Patrick Richards, G.F.S. Sirkett and Peter Wearing.

The photographs comprise a substantial portion of this work and gratitude is expressed to the following organisations for allowing reproduction of their material: Lloyds Bank Plc, The Bucks Herald, Times Newspapers Ltd, Coventry Evening Telegraph, Herts Adviser and Blists Hill Open Air Museum.

In addition the author is indebted to Arthur Barker Ltd for permission to reproduce the chapter on Lugano from the book Great Financial Disasters by Alex Murray and Mrs Bickel for permission to reproduce extracts from Flying, Banking and Music by Leslie E. Bickel, OBE.

The above acknowledgements relate to the 1989 edition. In compiling this second edition I am indebted to the following people who have assisted my enquiries: Alice Davies, Doreen Kennett, Roger Lord, Karen Sampson and Emma Stopford. Many thanks go to Lloyds Trade Union (LTU) who subsidized the printing of this book. The union is the largest independent trade union representing staff working in Lloyds Banking Group. In large parts of the Bank, LTU represents over 85% of all managers and staff.

The sources of the photographs and illustrations are as follows:

Drusilla Armitage   118b
Author   23a, 42–51, 60, 104, 107a, 144ab, 145ab, 148b, 147a, 151b, 152ab
Aylesbury Museum   11a
Mrs E.G.Brookes   102-3
Doreen Budgett   20
Herts Advertiser   122b
Keystone Press Agency   141
R. Kipling   98
Lloyds Bank Archivist   2, 11b, 13, 16, 19, 21–2, 23b, 29, 34, 36–41, 53–9, 61–71, 73–7, 88, 90-2, 94–7, 101, 108–9, 112–3, 114b, 151a, 156
Lloyds Bank News   72, 86, 99–100, 107b, 111, 119–120, 143ab
Stella Lowen   93
Penfold Photographic Archives   146
Deanna Plummer   145a
Janet Pusey   114a, 115–7
John Roberts   105–6, 110
The Bucks Herald   118a, 122a, 142ab
The Staff Magazine   28
Peter Webb   147

(a: above; b: below)

Origins of Banking

When civilization was in its infancy, traders used to barter with goods. Bartering became much simpler once a standard measure for the value of objects was established. One of the earliest was cattle. Later various kinds of metal, particularly iron, silver and gold became the more usual items of barter. Gold eventually became the universal currency and was used to pay armies and to purchase goods from other countries. The noblemen and kings often had to pay in advance for their luxury goods or armies. They therefore needed to borrow money and the earliest function of a banker was to lend money in return for interest.

Religion was a powerful influence in medieval feudal society. The Christian Church taught that it was wrong to lend money and charge interest or usury as it was called in those days. To charge usury was to sin against God. Banking was therefore left to the non-Christian communities as the Catholic Church forbad interest payments. The Jews became the earliest money-lenders and bankers to Europe because they were dispersed throughout many European countries. The religious objections to usury were eventually relaxed by medieval governments. Legislation so far lagged behind reality, that in England as late as 1552 an Act of Parliament prohibited all taking of interest as 'a vice most odious and detestable'. At length, in 1571, this Act was repealed and the charging of interest ceased to be a criminal offence provided the interest did not exceed 10 per cent. In 1854 the Usury Laws were finally repealed. Consequently, international banking became a respectable profession.

By the 14th century, the Lombardy state in northern Italy had become the centre of world trade. Ships departed from Genoa and Venice to Arabia, India and China bringing back such precious goods as silks and spices which were sold for huge profits. Many merchants in Lombardy became bankers because they provided the finance to build ships and pay for the voyages. In return for this finance they charged a very high rate of interest on their loans. The Lombardy merchants helped trade by writing notes or bills of exchange for the money owed for goods, to be paid within three months. The note or bill was sent to the buyer who accepted it by signing. It was then returned to the merchant who took it to his banker who accepted it by signing the note. The merchant was then able to exchange the note with other merchants for goods. Alternatively it could be sold to the banker who would pay the value of the bill less interest charges. The bill would be collected in full when the buyer finally paid the merchant.

The bankers in Lombardy eventually extended their operations overseas. This is why the main banking street in London is known as Lombard Street after the Italian money-lenders who settled there during the 13th and 14th centuries. They moved to London to be near the merchants whose trade they were helping to finance. From the Italian word 'bancos' is derived the word banker. Bancos means the benches on which the Italian merchants carried out their transactions in the 14th century. When a Lombardy banker was unable to meet the bills he had agreed to accept the other bankers would break his bench. From this we get the word 'bankrupt' used to describe someone who cannot pay his debts.

Some merchants specialised in holding and storing gold. They built the equivalent of the modern strongroom for holding gold and became known as goldsmiths. These goldsmiths issued a note of receipt which was in effect a promise to repay the depositor when he wanted his gold returned. These receipts became the first bank notes. In order to pay for goods, merchants wrote notes which requested their goldsmiths to pay traders a sum of money. These were in effect the first cheques. Sir Richard Martin was a goldsmith, money-lender, bullion dealer and warden of the Mint. It was at the Mint on 23 December 1580 that Sir Francis Drake delivered 23,000 lbs of silver and 100 lbs of gold bullion obtained during Drake's circumnavigation of the world the previous

September. Sir Richard and Sir Thomas Gresham, another goldsmith, both assisted in raising money for the Queen and in a re-coinage of 'Her Majesty's Money'. From these craftsmen – goldsmiths and money-lenders, sprung the goldsmith bankers of London from whom a number of the present day banks are descended.

Gold was imported by Spain from Latin America during the 16th century. The gold enabled Europe to have a reliable currency. This in turn led to a vast expansion of credit. Thus during the 15th and 16th centuries the first modern banks were established. One of which was the Banco di Santo Spirito in Rome, which is still in existence.

By the middle of the 17th century London had become the world's largest trading centre. The goldsmiths were taking large deposits from the big trading companies like the Hudson Bay Company and the East India Company in England. The goldsmiths were not large enough to finance the big trading ventures of the large companies or the heads of state who needed money in order to fight wars against other trading nations. In order to provide money for the state, the Bank of England was set up in 1694 specifically to finance King William III's war with Louis XIV of France. Its founders were to provide the Government with a loan of £1,200,000, the interest was to be £100,000 a year and the loan was to be repaid before 1706. The model of the great Continental banks of deposit was not followed in England as the Bank of England issued its own notes. The difference between the two is that banks of issue print their own notes, and they can lend money of their own creation to the extent that prudence permits, while deposit banks initially lend the money deposited with them to other borrowing customers. It was to be a long time before English bankers understood that deposit banking could be profitable even without the right of note issue. They eventually learned this fact as the Bank of England's notes increasingly drove their notes out of circulation. The Bank of England eventually became the only bank to issue its own notes in England.

During the 18th and 19th centuries the London banks led the world in becoming financiers and guarantors of trade. The banks used the money deposited with them to finance many foreign projects. Such international finance was used to start tea plantations in India, rubber groves in Malaysia and tramways in Tokyo. It is interesting to note that the railways, of Africa, Asia, Latin America and North America were built by companies financed or even owned by British banks.

The private bankers were not confined to London. Country banking developed only a little later than banking in London – probably as early as the middle of the 17th century. The country bankers were merchants of various kinds who like the goldsmiths developed banking as a subsidiary business although they had no previous experience with money. They were helped by the industrial revolution. With this came the need for capital on a scale previously unknown. Cash was required not only to develop an industry but to keep it going from week to week to meet expenses such as wages. Since banking facilities were not readily available everywhere it was left to the manufacturers to start their own banks. An example in North Wales was the cotton manufacturers S. & J. Knight who founded the Mold Bank in 1823. The originators of the private banks were not confined to industrialists but were also landowners or solicitors or anyone who had money.

Taylors and Lloyds, in common with other country banks, invested a sizeable part of their funds in overseas ventures. In 1817 they were holders of American bonds and by 1821 had added Russian, Prussian and French stocks. The bank also became heavily involved in the cotton trade with America, buying raw cotton in New York from where it was shipped to Liverpool and sold at the local market.

Unfortunately from the beginning of the 18th century financial crises were becoming more common. Each crisis was accompanied by bank failures. The crisis in 1825, the most severe yet, caused 73 of the country's principal banks to stop payment. In order to strengthen existing banking partnerships the Government decided in 1826 to allow the formation of joint stock banks.

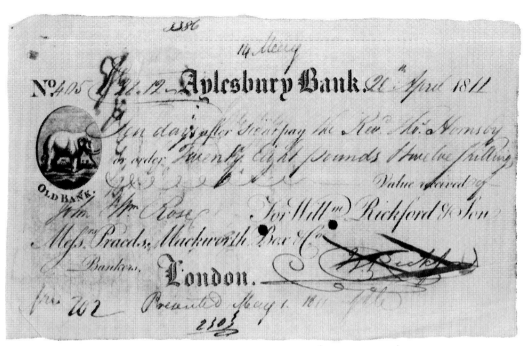

Aylesbury Bank post bill dated 20 April 1811 drawn by Willm Rickford & Son (bankers) on Messr Praeds, Mackworth, Box & Co, London (bankers). Being drawn at 10 days sight there was time to stop payment if stolen in the post. Country banks like William Rickford & Son had agents in London as they needed clearing facilities for the notes of other issues and transfer and payment facilities for their own customers.

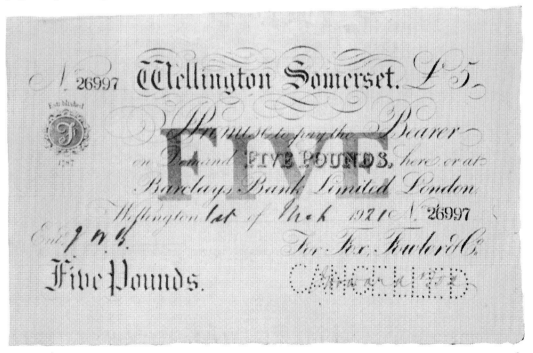

This banknote is one of the last hundred of such notes issued by Fox, Fowler and Co, the last of the English Private Banks entitled to issue its own notes. This right of issue was held by the Fox family continuously for 135 years from 1787 to 1921. This bank was originally founded by Thomas Fox, a woollen manufacturer, on the 30 October 1787 with the title of Fox and Co, Wellington. In 1921 Fox, Fowler & Co amalgamated with Lloyds Bank.

Banking after 1826

Banking in Britain in the early part of the 19th century was practised by firms rather than companies and was carried on in a small way by numerous private partnerships limited to six individuals. The partners tended to their banking trade alongside their various commercial ventures. Out of the London private banks and country private banks has grown the clearing banks that we know today.

After 1826 the formation of joint stock banks with publicly quoted shares was possible. The 1826 Act enabled banking partnerships of any number of members to be formed if more than 65 miles from London, the latter provision being intended to protect the Bank of England. The first of these new joint stock banks was the Lancaster Banking Company in 1827. Within ten years there were a hundred such banks in operation. Many were smaller than the private banks and it was the later Act of 1833 which made joint stock banking permissible throughout the United Kingdom, which in turn made possible the growth of the big commercial banks that we know today. The managers of these joint stock banks had to control large networks of branch offices. Gradually the old private bankers were absorbed by these new joint stock banks. Offices were opened in areas where banking had not existed before.

The term 'banker' was used to describe private bankers before the mid-19th century. From then onwards the ordinary managers and senior managers in the joint stock banks described themselves as bankers. In 1842, *Punch* described bank clerks as 'the hardest worked, worst paid and most polite body of men in the metropolis'. The Bank of England had its share of staff problems in the 1840s, as it was then announced 'that the Authorities had seen a disposition upon the part of certain Bank clerks to wear moustaches; that they strongly disapproved of the practice, and that if this hint be not attended to, measures will be resorted to which may prove of a painful nature'.

In the middle of the 19th century banking was a labour-intensive business. Large numbers of male clerks were supervised by a relatively small band of chief clerks and managers. Training depended heavily upon word-of-mouth instruction with very few books on banking available. The first library for banking staff was opened in 1850 by the Bank of England for its own clerks. The other banks slowly followed suit. The clerks, learning by experience, could work for up to six years before their practical education was complete.

In 1850 a clerk could expect to have a starting salary of £50 which would eventually rise to £250 per annum over 20 or 30 years. Many clerks with these low salaries were continually in debt especially as their salaries were paid quarterly in arrears. In 1857 it was reported in the *Bankers Magazine*: 'I do not say that a man and wife cannot live on £80 per annum. It may be done . . . by people who live on brick floors, who dress in fustian, who scour their own doorsteps, take their toad-in-the-hole to the baker on Sundays, eat cold bacon on other days when there is any in the cupboard, and a herring and potatoes when there is not; but it is not done by gentlemen who put on a clean shirt and an "all-rounder" (collar) every other morning.'

Prior to 1840 banks, and also insurance companies, required employees in a position of trust to provide personal sureties or guarantors. This was necessary in the case of embezzlement or fraud by the employee. The guarantees were, for example, £100 for messengers, £1,000 for clerks and £5,000 for managers. After 1840 the introduction of the fidelity guarantee insurance by the Guarantee Society helped overcome the drawback of the surety system.

By 1860 cheques were rapidly replacing banknotes at the counter as the most common medium of exchange. The growth of bank deposits made the rediscounting of bills of exchange less important to the bank as a source of earnings. Bank loans and overdrafts on customers accounts necessitated bank clerks and managers to acquire an

Bucks and Oxon Union Bank, Aylesbury.

HOUSE RULES.

The Manager in Residence shall have the entire charge and control of the House and Servants.

HOURS :—

BREAKFAST will be served at half-past Seven; DINNER at One; and TEA at Five, in the Dining Room, (A 1.)

SUPPER to be served at half-past Eight, in the Clerks' Common Room. (C 20.)

The House Door to be finally closed at Ten, and the Key placed in charge of the Manager in Residence.

CLERKS :—

The Clerks in Charge will undertake their Duty for one Month in rotation in the order of their standing; and hold themselves during such period at call at all Hours.

Each Clerk will sleep in the Accountant's Office for one Calendar Month in the order of the House List; and before retiring to Bed is required to inspect the Safes, Closets, Office Fittings, Trap and Front Doors, and satisfy himself that the Fastenings to the same remain as when left at the close of Business.

He shall also ascertain the safety of all Office Lights and Fires; and shall burn a Night Light in the Accountant's Office.

Leave of absence must not be applied for during the Month on Duty, or on Night-guard in the Accountant's Office.

HOUSE :—

The Dining Room shall be used for the purpose of Meals only; access there to to be by the Office Staircase.

The Clerks to occupy their Common Room, and their allotted Bed Rooms when not sleeping in the Accountant's Office.

The remainder of the House to be appropriated to the Manager, his Family and Servants exclusively; and the respective Fastenings to be in his charge.

SMOKING is not allowed in the House.

HOLIDAYS :—

Leave of absence will be granted from and after the Month of May in each Year as follows :——

To Managers, Accountant, and Clerks in Charge, from Saturday Evening until the commencement of Business on that day Fortnight.

And to Junior Clerks, from the same period until the commencement of Business on the Saturday next ensuing.

A Week must be allowed to intervene between each term of absence.

The Manager in Residence is charged with the due maintenance and observance of the above Regulations.

(By Order of the Board of Directors.)

BUCKS AND OXON UNION BANK.
AYLESBURY, 1st JULY, 1853.

Bucks and Oxon Union Bank, House Rules, 1853.

expertise in the evaluation and control of securities. The work of the London banks was also changed by the expanding market in the acceptance of foreign bills which demanded a knowledge of international shipping documents and special book-keeping skills.

In the 1890s, the supply of clerks was plentiful. This enabled the banks to pick and choose their recruits and insist upon a minimum standard of proficiency. Entry exams in arithmetic and English were set by many of the banks with the London and County Bank offering an optional examination for those clerks who were keen to 'single themselves out for future promotion'.

The bank amalgamations of the 1890s concentrated banking into the hands of a relatively small number of joint stock banks all with London headquarters and branch networks. By 1900 the National Provincial Bank with 240 branches had been joined in London by Lloyds Bank with 278 branches and the London City and Midland Bank with over 280 branches. They absorbed many of the provincial banks owned by local wealthy landed families. Many of them were Quakers who, because they had been persecuted, had established a tradition of mutual trust and financial prudence. Barclays, the last major joint stock bank to be created, was formed from the amalgamation of Quaker banks whose families dominated the board and took turns as chairman. With their local interest and caution they lent to customers in the surrounding area and left foreign lending to the private or merchant banks.

The more depositors the banks had, the greater the risk that a temporary panic could cause a run on the bank thus putting it out of business. With the spread of joint stock banks the risk became greater and with the growing scope for speculation crashes were inevitable. One famous crash was that of the very respected London firm of Overend Gurney. This crash reverberated through the world and compelled the Bank of England to become the 'lender of last resort'.

In May 1909 the *Bankers Magazine* stated: 'With the gradual absorption of country banks by the great joint stock institutions, the most important part of the business of banking – the lending of the bank's funds – has become centralised in the advance department at the head office of each bank, so that the managers and chief officials at the branches have been relieved of much of their responsibility. The natural result has been a reduction in the salaries paid . . . . one effect of the modern centralisation of banking had been to limit greatly the numbers of those who will in fact rise to well-paid posts.'

However, the changes did bring some compensations to ordinary bank clerks. The proliferation of branch offices meant more clerks were promoted to manager or accountant in the new offices. Pension schemes were introduced. In 1912 the Institute of Bankers acquired a sanatorium at Easthampstead, Berkshire. The sanatorium was equipped to treat tuberculosis patients and the Institute was able to reserve places for the employees of the banks. There was also a continuing reduction of working hours. Since 1886 banks had shut at 2.30 pm on a Saturday but from 1902 Saturday closing was fixed at 1.00 pm.

During the First World War the need for troops depleted the pre-war staff of the banks by between 30 and 40 per cent. The banks encouraged the formation of the 'Bankers Battalion' which was called the 26th (Service) Battalion of the Royal Fusiliers (Bankers). The battalion of 1,000 officers and men consisted 95 per cent of men recruited from the banks. Between May 1916 and the end of the war the battalion saw action in France and Italy.

The gaps left by the enlisted men were filled by temporary junior clerks, bank pensioners and by female clerks. Before the war banks appointed only a very small number of female clerks as telephonists or typists. Most of the secretarial work was done by male staff. In 1911 women formed only one per cent of the total banking workforce (476 out of 40,179 bank clerks). The war changed all this and, for example, by 1918 women and girls comprised 29 per cent of the staff of Lloyds Bank.

By 1918 about 300 bank absorptions and amalgamations had taken place with more than half of these having taken place in the last 50 years. As a result of these mergers the number of private banks fell from 37 in 1891 to 6 and the number of English joint stock banks fell from 106 to 34 during the same period. There was now a private understanding between the government and the banks which allowed the continued absorption of the small banks but did not permit the merging of any of the 'Big Five' banks. These five banks consisted of Barclays, Lloyds, Midland, National Provincial and Westminster. After 1918 further amalgamations of these banks had to receive Treasury and Board of Trade consent.

During the 1930s the coming of mechanization and the effects of the Depression meant that the banks who would normally take on 10 clerks were now only taking on five. With the monotonous work being done by female clerks on machines, the male clerks were expected to have a much higher standard of intelligence. All candidates for banking were now expected to have reached school matriculation standard and most banks had their own internal qualifying examinations. Lloyds, Midland, Martins, the National Bank and the Yorkshire Penny Bank recognized a 'common entrance' exam in arithmetic, English composition and geography. These exams were supervised by the City of London College. Career development was slow with even the most promising employee having to wait several years for promotion to a responsible post.

Many thousands of employees left the banks to take part in World War II. By early 1942, 23,000 bank employees or nearly 50 per cent of the pre-war staff of the banks had volunteered or been called up. The Kennet Committee which investigated the manpower resources of banks and insurance companies in 1942 revealed that 1,745 branches out of a total of 8,469 branch offices had been closed due to the release of bank officials for war service. By 1945 very few fit men under the age of 41 remained and the clerical force consisted of married women, bank pensioners and temporary junior clerks. Female employees had increased to over 20,000.

After the war men began to return to banking. However, with fewer men around due to the effects of war and the lower birth-rate of the early 1930s the banks had difficulty in recruiting young men. In addition more young men now went to university and many other opportunities outside banking were available to those who did not wish to continue with their full-time education.

In contrast women were attracted into banking. In Lloyds Bank their numbers doubled between 1946 and 1960. By 1963, for the first time, there were more women than men in the Bank. Women were originally employed as typists or clerks but they were gradually given more responsible posts. By 1968 almost half the 6,000 Lloyds' cashiers were women and there were 64 women with 'chief general manager's' appointments and eight with board appointments. In 1970 Lloyds appointed its first woman branch manager.

Job titles have changed over the years. Gone are the days when a bank had clerks, technical and services staff and managers with self-explanatory titles. Today there is a bewildering array of job titles and departments such as Chief Manager, Research and Standards, Planning and Liaison Department and Technical Officer, Domestic Systems Department.

Clearing House, Post Office Court, Lombard Street, 1902. By 1770 the cheque system had developed in London with customers paying in cheques drawn on other banks. The bank clerks found it easier to meet at one central point than go round each bank individually exchanging cheques for cash. The clerks originally used to meet at a chop house called the Five Bells *in* Dove Court *off Lombard Street where the exchange of cheques would take place. The difference in totals between the banks would be settled in cash. The Clearing House was founded by private bankers and it was not until 1854 that the joint stock banks were admitted. In those days there were no machines to sort the cheques.*

WITH *this Bank have been incorporated the undermentioned Companies and Firms :—*

In 1865, Lloyds & Co., Birmingham Old Bank (established 1765)
„ Moilliet & Sons, Birmingham
„ P. & H. Williams, Wednesbury Old Bank
In 1866, Stevenson, Salt & Co., Stafford Old Bank (established 1737)
„ Warwick and Leamington Banking Co.
In 1868, A. Butlin & Son, Rugby Old Bank (established 1791)
In 1872, R. & W. F. Fryer, Wolverhampton Old Bank
In 1874, Shropshire Banking Company
In 1879, Coventry and Warwickshire Banking Company
In 1880, Beck & Co., Shrewsbury and Welshpool Old Bank
In 1884, Barnetts, Hoares & Co., London (established about 1677)
„ Bosanquet, Salt & Co., London (established 1796)
In 1888, Pritchard, Gordon & Co., Broseley and Bridgnorth
In 1889, Birmingham Joint Stock Bank Limited
„ Worcester City and County Banking Co. Limited
In 1890, Wilkins & Co., Old Bank, Brecon, Cardiff, etc. (established 1778)
„ Beechings & Co., Tunbridge Wells, Hastings, etc.
In 1891, Praeds & Co., London (established 1802)
„ Cobb & Co., Margate, etc. (estab. 1785)
„ Hart, Fellows & Co., Nottingham (established 1808)
In 1892, R. Twining & Co., London (estab. 1824)
„ Bristol & West of England Bank Ltd.
In 1893, Curteis, Pomfret & Co., Rye (established 1790)
„ Herries, Farquhar & Co., London (established 1770)
In 1894, Bromage & Co., Old Bank, Monmouth (established 1819)
In 1895, Paget & Co., Leicester Bank (estab. 1825)
In 1897, County of Gloucester Bank Limited
„ Williams & Co., Chester, etc. (established 1792)

In 1898, Jenner & Co., Sandgate and Shorncliffe Bank
In 1899, Burton Union Bank Limited
„ Stephens, Blandy & Co., Reading, etc. (established 1790)
In 1900, Vivian, Kitson & Co., Torquay Bank (established 1832)
„ Liverpool Union Bank Limited
„ Cunliffes, Brooks & Co., Manchester, etc. (established 1792)
„ Brooks & Co., London
„ William Williams Brown & Co., Leeds (established 1813)
„ Brown, Janson & Co., London (established 1813)
In 1902, Bucks and Oxon Union Bank Limited
„ Pomfret, Burra & Co., Ashford Bank (established 1791)
In 1903, Hodgkin, Barnett & Co., Newcastle-upon-Tyne, etc.
„ Grant and Maddison's Union Banking Co. Limited
In 1905, Hedges, Wells & Co., Wallingford Bank (established 1813)
In 1906, Devon and Cornwall Banking Company Limited
In 1908, Lambton & Co., Newcastle-upon-Tyne, etc. (established 1788)
In 1909, David Jones & Co., Llandovery, etc. (established 1800)
In 1911, Hill & Sons, West Smithfield, E.C., etc. (established 1825)
In 1912, Peacock, Willson & Co., Sleaford, etc. (established 1792)
In 1914, Wilts & Dorset Banking Co., Ltd. (established 1835)
In 1918, The Capital & Counties Bank, Limited (established 1834)
In 1919, West Yorkshire Bank Limited (established 1829)
In 1921, Fox, Fowler & Co., Wellington (Som.), etc. (established 1787)
In 1923, Cox & Co., London, etc. (established 1758)
„ Henry S. King & Co. London, etc. (established 1816)

Lloyds Bank list of incorporated companies and firms showing takeover and mergers prior to 1923. By this time some 50 banks had been absorbed. Many of the banks taken over had absorbed banks themselves resulting in Lloyds having a direct or indirect title to nearly 200 constituent banks in all.

Development of Lloyds Bank

In June 1765 the private firm of Taylors and Lloyds opened for business at Dale End, Birmingham. The partnership consisted of Sampson Lloyd (Sampson Lloyd II), John Taylor, Sampson Lloyd junior (III) and John Taylor junior, each of whom provided one quarter of the £8,000 capital. Of the four original partners John Taylor and Sampson Lloyd II are the best remembered. John Taylor was a button-maker and Unitarian and Sampson Lloyd was an ironmaker and Quaker. Unlike some bankers they did not continue with their original business alongside their new business. In the title of the bank, 'Taylors and Lloyds', the name of the Taylor partner came first probably because he was wealthier and better known in Birmingham. However, the other main partner, Sampson Lloyd II was the inspiration of the bank with the result that the bank is now known as Lloyds Bank.

This private bank had only one office situated in Birmingham. There was no branch system such as we know today. The office at Dale End, Birmingham, remained until around 1840 when there was a move to High Street, Birmingham. The association with Taylors ended in 1852. Much of the stability of the partnership was due to the Quaker tradition of prudence and moderation. However, in order to survive it was necessary to broaden its capital basis. This was accomplished in 1865 when the failure of the rival Birmingham bank of Attwood, Spooner & Co prompted Lloyds & Co to turn into a joint stock bank. A merger with another local bank, Moilliet and Sons took place and the new joint bank was known as Lloyds Banking Company Limited. This new company had an authorised capital of £2m, seven offices and 50 staff servicing 4,524 accounts. Its board included Joseph Chamberlain, who later became a famous Cabinet Minister.

There now began a period of rapid growth with branches opening in many areas including Oldbury (1864) and Tamworth (1865). By the 1880s the Bank had established itself as a powerful banking force in the Midlands. The Bank now turned its attention towards London when in 1884 it absorbed the London business of Messrs Barnetts, Hoares, Hanbury & Lloyd, a descendant of Hanbury, Taylor, Lloyd & Bowmans Bank, which had been started in 1771 by the sons of the original Birmingham partners. Another London firm was also absorbed in 1884 and the new bank was known as Lloyds, Barnetts and Bosanquets Bank Ltd. In 1889 the title was changed to Lloyds Bank Ltd.

This acquisition brought about the connection of Lloyds Bank with the black horse. The Bank's first symbol was a beehive which had been introduced in the 1820s as a distinguishing mark for banknotes. In heraldry it is the emblem of industry. With the amalgamation Lloyds inherited the Lombard Street sign of the black horse which had a direct descent from a goldsmith known as Humphrey Stokes or Stocks who first used it as his trading sign. This goldsmith is mentioned in the oldest printed list of London merchants and bankers, which was published in 1677, as keeping 'Running Cashes'. Today's equivalent would be current accounts. Following several changes of name and amalgamations this business became part of Messrs Barnetts, Hoares, Hanbury and Lloyd. By 1910 all head office business had been transferred from Birmingham to 71 Lombard Street and the black horse became more representative of the new location, although the beehive was also used until 1930.

Mergers with other banks continued. One bank which was taken over in 1893, Herries Farquhar & Co, had the distinction of originating travellers cheques. In 1914 the merger with the Wilts and Dorset Bank added another 100 offices. By the start of the First World War in 1914, the Bank had nearly 900 offices and over half a million customers. In 1918 the acquisition of Capital and Counties Bank meant 473 offices were added to the branch structure. In 1918 total accounts were less than a million, spread over 1,273 offices in England and Wales serviced by 11,400 bank staff of whom under a third were women.

By 1969 accounts had increased to over 4½ million spread over 2,307 offices serviced by 32,500 staff of whom more than half were women. This growth was helped by further amalgamations. In February 1921 the amalgamation with Fox, Fowler & Co took place. It is interesting to note that this acquisition marked the end of the last private bank note issue in England and Wales. In 1923 Cox & Co were absorbed. This bank was agent and banker to the Army. By now there had been 50 direct takeovers.

Lloyds was now one of the 'Big Five' banks. The Bank had already taken an interest in the international role of banking by acquiring in 1911 the Paris and Le Havre business of Armstrong & Co. This was renamed Lloyds Bank (France). From 1917, the bank was run jointly by Lloyds and National Provincial Foreign Bank. In 1955 Lloyds acquired full ownership and it was renamed Lloyds Bank (Foreign). Later its name was changed to Lloyds Bank Europe.

In 1918 Lloyds Bank had taken an interest in South America by acquiring the London & River Plate Bank. This Bank was merged in 1923 with the London and Brazilian Bank to form the Bank of London and South America, which was known as BOLSA. In 1971 Lloyds Bank bought a controlling interest in BOLSA and merged it with Lloyds Bank Europe to form Lloyds and Bolsa International Bank. This title changed in 1974 to Lloyds Bank International known as LBI. In January 1986 LBI was merged with the clearing bank.

Back in 1967 Lloyds Bank had bought Lewis's Bank from Martins. Founded in 1928, with its head office in Liverpool, Lewis's Bank consisted of ten branches, in Lewis's department stores. It was merged with Lloyds Bank by Act of Parliament in 1981. In 1968 both Lloyds and Barclays made a bid for Martins Bank. A merger had been considered between Barclays, Lloyds and Martins but this had been blocked by the Monopolies Commission. As Barclays made the higher bid, Martins joined with Barclays, leaving Lloyds Bank the smallest of the 'Big Four'.

During the 1970s the bank continued developing its international side. In 1974 the American First Western Bank and Trust Company was acquired and renamed Lloyds Bank California (LBC). Prior to this in 1966 the bank had acquired total control of The National Bank of New Zealand. The idea of a Lloyds Bank Group had now been realized with offices in nearly 50 countries. At home Access was launched in October 1972 in conjunction with National Westminster Bank and Midland Bank. In 1973, with all its branches computerised, the first automated teller machine was introduced which we know today as Cashpoint.

In the 1980s with the rapid advances in technology and international banking it became important to have a single international image. By the end of 1985 Lloyds Bank group had become a £43 billion group operating about 3,000 offices in 49 countries and employing nearly 70,000 people. The time was right to form one unified bank. This was achieved in January 1986 when LBI was merged with the clearing bank to form Lloyds Bank Plc with the black horse as the world-wide logo. LBC was sold to Sanwa Bank and a controlling interest was bought in the Continental Bank of Canada. A merchant bank was created with its headquarters at the former head office of LBI in Queen Victoria Street.

At home in 1982 it was decided to form a chain of estate agencies. This idea was regarded by some people as innovative and by others as highly speculative. The bank acquired its first agency, Charles Hawkins and Son in East Anglia and displayed the black horse logo. Today, Black Horse Agencies have over 500 offices to meet all the financial needs of the homebuyer and the idea has been copied by other financial institutions. Lloyds Bank Commercial Service was set up to meet the special needs of the medium sized company and now has 60 offices covering the major towns and cities throughout the country.

Lloyds Bank has built its business by providing a service to individual customers. Some famous customers who banked with Lloyds and its constituent banks have included Louis Napoleon who was Emperor Napoleon III from 1852–1870, the Duke of Wellington who won the battle of Waterloo in 1815 and Sir Winston Churchill. A portrait of Nell Gwyn graces the elegant interior of Private Banking and Trust branch in Grosvenor Street, London. This fine building, completed in 1724, was acquired by the Bank in 1986. Nell Gwyn's grandson the second Duke of St Albans was one of its first residents. The branch provides a very special service to its eminent customers. Services include the individual care of an Account Executive, who advises on and deals with all their financial affairs – from arranging their children's education to planning their estates and portfolio management, trust planning and property investment. International customers visiting London can even have theatre tickets booked for them.

Lloyds Bank is the smallest and most profitable of the high street banks with an estimated five million customers against Midland's 5.7 million and Barclays, and National Westminster's seven million each. The customers of today are far more demanding than they were in 1765 when the private firm of Taylors & Lloyds opened for business. Today's customers are more selective and adventurous. As technology advances they want new products and new delivery systems. They demand better quality and greater value for money. New concepts are being developed to help change the image of the Bank to its retail customers. These include additional LobbyService and Personal Service offices with automatic cashiers and open-plan branches with shop-fronts and interiors that reflect the ideas of modern retailing. One wonders what John Taylor and Sampson Lloyd would make of today's banking world.

Advertisement from the Bankers' Almanac and Year Book 1920/21 showing the black horse and beehive logo of Lloyds Bank. Sculptured stone beehives were a feature of many branches of Lloyds Bank up to the early 1930s. This symbol can still be seen incorporated in the outside walls of branches in many towns, especially in the Midlands.

Frederick Partridge Esq - Depositor -

in account with

Lloyds Bank Limited.

Solihull.

Dr.					Cr.				
1930					1930				
Mar 18	Forward	167	10	5	Mar 26	Forward H.O. Sa.	242	17	5
22	Self	6	6			a/c	11		7
29	a/c	6	6		Apr 9	a/c	47	11	
31	a/c, Imd.	25			24	a/c	10	2	
Apr 4	Self	10			29	a/c	49	9	8
12	a/c	6	6						
16	Power	3							
17	Self	9							
28	Austen	11	8	9					
		269	19	2			371	9	3

Accounts were recorded in pass-books, issued by the Bank, kept by the customer, and entries were made by clerks in the branch. Statements, like we know today, were not common until after the Second World War.

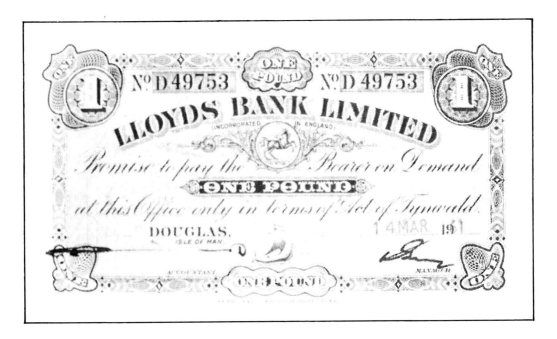

One of the last £1 banknotes issued by Lloyds Bank in the Isle of Man. Until December 1961 all the major banks had separate note issues for their Manx branches. In December 1961, with the Lloyds Bank issue at £4,000, the Manx Government assumed sole responsibility for the local note issue. Douglas branch to this very day is compelled to keep a record of all banknotes in circulation, although being collectors' pieces none are ever returned. Records show that in 1976 there were 865 notes outstanding with the then collector's value of approximately £10 each. The notes were all signed by the manager and accountant of Douglas branch.

H.O. NEWS

No. 1

March 1966

Lloyds Bank plays a Trump Card

Credit cards of one kind or another have been much in the news lately. The recently announced Bankers Card will be widely welcomed. It is an advance on those already introduced. Bankers Cards will be available to approved customers of Lloyds Bank, Martins Bank, Williams Deacon's Bank, The National Bank, Yorkshire Bank, Glyn Mills & Co., Lewis's Bank, Bank of Scotland, Royal Bank of Scotland, National Commercial Bank of Scotland, Bank of Ireland and Hibernian Bank without distinction.

They will enable the holder to have his cheque up to £30 readily accepted at shops, hotels, restaurants, travel agents, etc., throughout the country, and to cash a cheque at any of the 4,600 branches of any of the banks without charge and with no delay.

The use of Bankers Cards will be of special benefit to customers travelling away from home. It will also overcome the reluctance of some customers to offer their cheques to shopkeepers who do not know them.

New Products

Banking is an intensely competitive business. We are all of us trying all the time both to improve our existing services to customers and to devise new ones that are likely to be of real benefit.

So far as new products are concerned it is not necessarily a good thing to be the first to offer them. In the long run it's research and thoroughness that pay off, rather than novelty.

A great deal of research and organisation has been put into the Scheme for Bankers Cards and it has been well worth taking a little time to secure their acceptability by so many Banks.

We aren't always first but we are always best.

The Take Over Bid

Our new subsidiary

On Thursday 27th January, the papers carried our bald announcement that offers had been accepted in respect of 91.4% of the shares of the NBNZ Ltd. affected, and that the offer was therefore unconditional. The take-over was going ahead.

But it didn't say that on the Tuesday morning only a minority had accepted .... They had! Most of the acceptances arrived on the Wednesday. There was never any real fear that the offer might fail, of course. The truth is that the large institutional holders seldom do accept such an offer until the last moment. Why do so when they've nothing to gain by prompt acceptance and everything to lose in the unlikely event of a better offer coming from somewhere else? Anyway, they did accept. Indeed, we now hold acceptances for 96.3% of the shares involved. Who owns the few shares for which no acceptances have been received? .. Possibly old ladies who haven't yet [illegible] Investment Management Service, or estates of deceased uncles for which probate has not yet been granted, or people who haven't notified their change of address. They'll all be looked after.

Why buy the New Zealand Bank?

The acquisition of the share capital of The National Bank of New Zealand Limited is part of the bank's policy of strengthening our links in the Commonwealth.

The NBNZ is a successful and profitable business with 189 branches throughout New Zealand. We have had cordial relations with this bank for very many years and this new development will bring it as closely into the Lloyds Bank family as Lloyds Bank Europe Limited.

We also have substantial interests in the following:

Bank of London & South America Ltd., National & Grindlays Bank Ltd., National Commercial Bank of Scotland Ltd., Bowmaker Ltd., Lloyds & Scottish Ltd.

'On-line' Computer System

We have been using computers for a long time now. Some are installed in the Clearings Sections and in the Registrar's Department in Worthing. But of more dramatic interest are those employed on ledger and statement posting.

We now have two Computer Centres concentrating on this work – one in the West End of London and one in the City. The City Computer Centre will be progressively transferred later this year to a new building erected over Cannon Street Station, which has been leased by the Bank. An additional Computer Centre is planned for Birmingham.

The new building at Cannon Street Station which will soon house our City Computer Centre.

Already most branches in the London area have their accounts posted by a computer. Branches in Croydon, Guildford, Brighton and Portsmouth have been linked up this year, and we have a massive programme for extending this operation throughout the country during 1966-1968.

The System

We were the first British bank to announce, in May last year, the introduction of a computer-controlled communication system. Key to the new system is the establishing of direct Teleprocessing links between the computer and branches. At the branch, details of all vouchers are recorded on punched paper tape which is produced as a by-product of a special listing machine. The tape is then fed into a terminal unit and the data is transmitted along private G.P.O. telephone lines under the control of a computer in London.

At the Computer Centre a control unit receives the information from the various branch terminals – any or all of which can be transmitting at one time – and stores it on a magnetic disc memory. A second computer then directs these entries to the current account records which are also held on other direct-access magnetic disc files.

This work continues throughout the day, together with such operations as the preparation of customers' statements. At the end of each day the computer prepares branch Management control information including lists of out-of-order accounts and up-to-date balances; these are despatched with customers' statements to reach the branches by the following morning.

The statement produced by the computer gives fuller narrative information of entries on customers' accounts, and has been extremely well received. Cheques will continue to be described by their serial numbers but other entries, including dividends and standing orders, will be identified by description.

Entries can be transmitted by each terminal point at speeds of up to 2,000 an hour, with an overall reception speed at the Computer Centre of some 20,000 entries an hour from all terminal points. The printers linked to the system produce 1,100 lines of print a minute. At this speed a customer's statement can be prepared in less than a second!

Punched paper tape containing all the required information for entries on customers' accounts is produced as a by-product of this listing machine at the distant branch. The tape is then fed into the Teleprocessing Unit (bottom right) which transmits the data instantaneously to the computer.

Information about Banking

The recently issued film about banking, "Money in the Bank", was produced on behalf of all the London Clearing Banks by the Banking Information Service.

This service is not widely known outside the newspaper world and readers may be interested to know what it is:

First of all, it has nothing whatever in common with our own Information Department: it does *not* provide commercial intelligence or reports on firms, nor is it concerned with credit-rating. It is, in fact, an auxiliary service set up by the London Clearing Banks and the Scottish Banks for the purpose of disseminating information about banking in general.

The present Chairman of the Banking Information Service is Mr. E. J. N. Warburton, our Director and Chief General Manager, and the Secretary is Mr. John Hunsworth, an experienced financial journalist. The offices are housed, appropriately enough, at 10 Lombard Street, in the same building as the Committee of London Clearing Bankers' Headquarters, the London Clearing House, the Institute of Bankers, and our own Public Relations Section.

The activities of the Banking Information Service are mainly to do with the press. It keeps newspapers and financial periodicals informed about developments in banking and receives and deals with enquiries from journalists everywhere about news on banking. It is, as it were, the Publicity and Public Relations department for banking as a whole. Collective advertising of Credit Transfers, for example, is handled by the Service.

Bank Education Service

Education on matters to do with banks is not a function of the Banking Information Service. But it *is* the purpose of the recently set up Bank Education Service. This, too, is an auxiliary of the Committee of London Clearing Bankers, with offices in the same building. It is headed by a noted educationalist as Director. It is the intention of this Service to co-operate with schools and other educational establishments in helping to teach young people more about the nature of money and banking.

The Service is publishing educational booklets for distribution to schools. The first four entitled "The Role of the Banks", "How to Handle Cheques", "The Movements of Notes and Coins" and "The Life Story of a Cheque", are already issued. Eventually a panel of lecturers will be available to give talks to school classes when invited to do so.

H.O. News

H.O. News is issued by the Public Relations Officer of Lloyds Bank. It is intended to help to keep branch staffs informed of what's going on in the Bank. It is hoped to issue it every few months.

An Interesting History

Professor R. S. Sayers' well-known "Lloyds Bank in the History of English Banking" is not a book you can pick up and read on the train. Yet the growth of our bank from its modest

beginnings in Birmingham more than 200 years ago makes a fascinating story – and one that arouses much interest in schools where 'projects' on banking history are undertaken.

So we are producing a 'potted history' in a full-colour paper-back – one that can be read right through in about half an hour.

When it is ready, copies will be sent to each branch. Extra copies can be had from Stationery Department. Look out for a B Circular in a few weeks.

Lloyds Bank Review

In its present form "Lloyds Bank Review" commenced publication in March 1930. For nine years it was a monthly, containing one signed article by a leading expert in his field, and notes and reports on current financial and economic topics. On the outbreak of the second world war, publication was suspended.

In 1946 publication of the "Review" was resumed as a quarterly. Since then it has usually contained three articles by acknowledged specialists in their subjects, and a statistical section. For many years the "Review" was edited by Mr. Alwyn Parker who had been a director of the Bank since 1919. In 1953 Mr. W. Manning Dacey, the Bank's Economic Adviser, was appointed Editor. After the death of Mr. W. Manning Dacey in 1964 Mr. J. R. Winton, the Bank's Assistant Economic Adviser, became Editor. Today the "Review" is probably the most influential of all bank reviews in this country. It is held in extremely high regard in financial, industrial and academic circles both at home and abroad.

At present about 22,000 copies of the "Review" are circulated, including some 4,000 overseas. Branch customers take some 11,000 copies and there is a large demand from universities, colleges, libraries and schools. A copy of each issue is sent to every M.P. and to all leading newspapers and periodicals.

First edition of H.O. News, *March 1966. This edition stated that the paper was issued by the Public Relations Officer of the Bank 'to keep branch staff informed of what's going on in the Bank' and 'it was hoped to issue it every few months'. The first few editions were printed in black ink on pink paper. In March 1967 the name was changed to* Lloyds Bank News *and it is now published every month in colour. Today the publication has its own staff with Tony Prior as editor. Monthly circulation is now over 52,000 copies.*

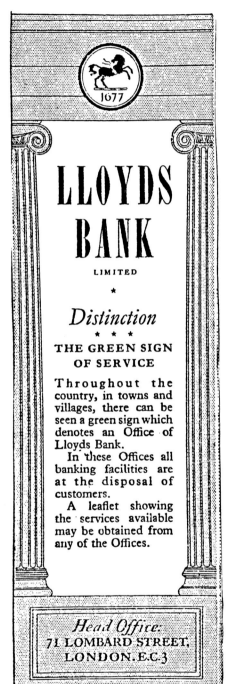

LLOYDS BANK
LIMITED

★

Distinction
★ ★ ★
THE GREEN SIGN OF SERVICE

Throughout the country, in towns and villages, there can be seen a green sign which denotes an Office of Lloyds Bank.

In these Offices all banking facilities are at the disposal of customers.

A leaflet showing the services available may be obtained from any of the Offices.

Head Office:
71 LOMBARD STREET,
LONDON, E.C.3

Leo McKern, actor, star of recent television commercials advertising the Bank's quality services. The shooting-party ad, featuring Leo McKern, was one of 15 winners from over 480 world-wide entries in the American Bank Marketing Association's 1986 Advertising Awards.

Press advert 1936, emphasising the green sign of service of Lloyds Bank. Until comparatively modern times bankers confined themselves to sober and modest announcements in the press. The advertisements of today, although conveying the same message, are much more sophisticated with colourful full page newspaper displays.

Lloyds Bank International

In January 1986, Lloyds Bank International (LBI) was merged with the clearing bank. It was originally formed in 1974 after becoming a wholly owned subsidiary of the Bank. Previous to this it was known as Lloyds & Bolsa International Bank with Lloyds Bank owning 51 per cent of the shares. The following banks form part of the history of LBI:

London & River Plate Bank

In 1862 in Argentina there were only a few hundred square miles of cultivated land with cereals being among the principal imports, and wool, hides, lard and other pastoral products being the chief exports. The opening up of the pampas and the transformation of Argentina into one of the granaries of the world was the work of military expeditions, the railways, the banks and the immigrants. George Drabble played a leading role in the establishment of the railway. He had originally come to Argentina from Manchester in the late 1840s to look after the interests of Drabble Bros, the family firm who exported cotton goods. He later became Chairman of the London and River Plate Bank. It is said that Anglo-Argentine co-operation began in 1862 when the London, Buenos Aires and River Plate Bank and the Buenos Aires Great Southern Railway were founded.

The London, Buenos Aires and River Plate Bank was incorporated on 27 September 1862 with its head office at 40 Moorgate, London. It opened its first branch in Buenos Aires on 1 January 1863. One of its earliest customers was General Urquiza, who had defeated Rosas, the dictator, at the Battle of Caseros, some ten years earlier. J. H. Green was the first manager and he was a merchant of long standing in Buenos Aires while de la Riestra, the Resident Director, had formerly been Finance Minister of the Province of Buenos Aires. It is interesting to note that when Mr Green arrived from England he bought with him two boxes of gold doubloons, accounts books and letters of credit. The latter enabled him to raise money on arrival thereby beginning business as soon as possible. Later steamers brought him additional bullion, scales to weigh coin, a copying press, safes and an enormous amount of stationery. The bank was a success and other branches soon followed in Rosario (1866) and Cordoba.

The branches were far away from the London Head Office and in 1863 the quickest mail-boat took over three weeks from England to the River Plate with the result that it was normally two months before Head Office could receive a reply to one of its letters.

The bank changed its name in 1865 to the London and River Plate Bank. A great deal of its business consisted in the financing of imports and exports. Gradually a network of agents and correspondents was established to handle the trade between the River Plate countries and Europe and the United States. Connections in Amsterdam, Hamburg, Genoa, Berlin, New York and St Petersburg were established. European branches were opened with a branch in Paris opening in 1885 to be followed by Lisbon and Antwerp. For a time the bank issued its own notes in several of its centres. Other banks also issued notes but it was the only bank to redeem its entire issue.

By 1891 the recession, which had begun in 1889, had caused many banks to close their doors to their customers and suspend payments. It has been estimated that three quarters of the banking capital in Argentina was lost during this crisis. However, the London and River Plate Bank was one of the few banking institutions in the country that survived the crash. Not only was the bank able to maintain 'business as usual' but its business actually increased during the year. In the same year it acquired the old established bank of Carabassa & Co and opened a branch in Rio de Janeiro, as well as agencies in New York and Paysandu in Uruguay.

In 1918 Lloyds Bank Ltd acquired control. This gave The London and River Plate Bank access to the wide connections in Great Britain and other countries where Lloyds Bank was represented.

London & Brazilian Bank

This bank was established in 1862 with the first branch opening in Rio de Janeiro in February 1863. Shortly afterwards branches were established in Bahia and Pernambuco and the Anglo-Portuguese Bank which had branches in Lisbon and Oporto was taken over.

In 1864 a severe monetary crisis in Brazil, followed in 1866 by the repercussions of the Overend Gurney crisis in London, hit the fortunes of the new bank. A run on the bank in May 1866 resulted in the Rio branch being drained of over a million pounds within 15 days. The bank only just survived. Head Office in London shipped gold to Rio as fast as possible. To obtain further funds the manager in Rio sold drafts on London to the value of £200,000. These events led eventually in 1871 to the bank being reorganised. The fortunes of the bank changed and by 1880 it had become the leading foreign bank in Brazil with a wide network of branches from Manaus on the Amazon and Para and Maranhao on the northern coast to Porto Alegre, Pelotas and Rio Grande do Sul in the south.

In the early days it was difficult to build up an adequate staff as there was no reserve of experienced men to fall back upon. In choosing their first managers Head Office in London preferred men with commercial rather than banking experience. Much business was done on a personal basis and the manager had to win the respect of the commercial community. Managers tended to stay at the same branch for a long time. For example, John Gordon spent in excess of 15 years at the Rio office. Managers had direct dealings with heads of state and finance ministers. They had to be able to stand up to an intimidating minister who threatened forced loans.

To help managers, staff were recruited from British domestic banks. They were given a contract which lasted usually three to five years. Their salaries were paid in sterling. Their main duty was to introduce and maintain the book-keeping systems as they knew all about branch banking. A scarcity of English staff led to Scotsmen being employed. They were well received as the Scottish banks issued their own notes and this valuable experience was of great value to the note issuing banks overseas. Local staff were recruited as cashiers, porters, bill collectors and watchmen.

Much of the success of this bank is due to one man, John Beaton, whose whole life was devoted to its service. In 1885 he was appointed managing director and in 1905 was elected chairman. He remained chairman until his ninetieth year, shortly before the amalgamation with the London and River Plate Bank in 1923. By this time the bank had offices in Buenos Aires, Rosario, Montevideo, Manchester, Paris, New York and also in Portugal.

Bank of London & South America

In 1923, Lloyds Bank brought about the amalgamation of the London and Brazilian Bank with the London and River Plate Bank. For many years these two banks had been friendly rivals in several Latin American republics and they shared a basic similarity in tradition and outlook. The new name chosen was that of Bank of London & South America Limited (BOLSA). The amalgamation of these two banks took several years to complete.

In 1936 BOLSA took over the Anglo-South American Bank known as the 'Anglo'. This bank had absorbed many banks itself. Its beginnings date from 1888 with the foundation of the Bank of Tarapaca and London. This particular bank was originally formed to finance the export of nitrates from Chile to the United Kingdom and Europe. The nitrate fields had been won for Chile by the War of the Pacific. The bank was founded largely on the initiative of Colonel North who came to South America to work for a Yorkshire firm of boiler-makers. He eventually acquired substantial interests in the nitrate industry and was an influential figure both in Chile and London.

BOLSA, which was now the sole British bank in Latin America, possessed an unrivalled network of branches and under the chairmanship of Sir Francis Glyn (1948–1957) major improvements were made. The bank, which had been under-capitalised, raised its capital in 1951 to over £5m by a further issue of shares and transferred £1m to the published reserves. New schemes for staff recruitment and training of management were introduced. A new London headquarters building was built at the intersection of Queen Victoria Street and Queen Street which replaced the cramped and unsatisfactory building in Tokenhouse Yard.

The bank in Buenos Aires followed in the footsteps of London in becoming 'computerised'. It established one of its new branches in a large department store. A campaign was launched to promote 'non-traditional' exports and it succeeded in introducing the credit card to Argentina.

During the chairmanship of Sir George Bolton (1957–70) BOLSA was transformed from a regional bank into an international bank transacting business throughout the world. The two fundamental decisions that changed the bank's policy were to move out of the sterling system and largely into that of the dollar and to regard the bank's major responsibility as due to the host countries. In 1960 the bank acquired the established merchant banking firm of Balfour, Williamson and Company Ltd, which was originally founded in Liverpool in 1851 by three Scotsmen.

Because the bank was based in London and operating mainly outside the sterling area it found that it needed a dollar partner. This partner was found in 1965, with the Mellon Bank and Trust Company of Pittsburgh. Through its subsidiary, Mellon Bank International, it acquired a 15 per cent stake in BOLSA which was later increased to 25 per cent in 1968. BOLSA now had fresh capital in convertible currency and its position in New York was enhanced by being associated with a bank that had powerful connections in the heartland of the US industry. The advantage for Mellon was that it had the benefit of BOLSA's wide connections for the expansion of its international business.

The bank was one of the first to recognise the potential of the London market in non-resident currencies which we know today as the Eurodollar market. It played an important part in the development of this market and the subsequent market for longer-term funds known as the Eurobond market.

As the bank's volume of business increased it became necessary to reorganise its head office structure which was originally designed to administer the traditional business of a British overseas bank. An International Banking Division was established with its own representatives in East and West Europe, and North America. Representative offices were established in Mexico City in 1968 and in Tokyo in 1969. The purchase of an equity in the old-established banque d'affaires, Banque Worms et Cie, helped its European connections. In England the Birmingham representative office was made into a branch and added to the provincial branches which existed in Bradford and Manchester.

The International Banking Division in London acquired expertise in the foreign currency financing of international trade and investment all over the world. In Spain it helped finance the steel industry and in Chile the bank aided the mining sector. Brazil was helped with the sale of aircraft, and the petroleum industry in Yugoslavia and petrochemical concerns in Argentina benefitted from finance.

Bank of London & Montreal

The funds available in Britain for investment overseas were largely devoted to the sterling Commonwealth countries. BOLSA wished to expand its business in the Caribbean and began looking for a suitable partner. Canada had long established commercial interests in the Caribbean. Its oldest bank, the Bank of Montreal, had close links with London because during the war it had provided assistance to the Bank of England.

On 3 July 1958, the Bank of London and Montreal (BOLAM) was established to explore the banking possibilities in the West Indies and develop the existing branch network that BOLSA already had in Central and South America. The Bank of Montreal provided fresh capital and the Bank of London & South America handed over its branches, business and experienced staff in Colombia, Ecuador, Venezuela, El Salvador, Nicaragua & Guatemala. The new bank opened its head office in Nassau, Bahamas, in October 1958 and soon established itself in Trinidad, Jamaica, Honduras and Panama. In Venezuela the branch in Caracas was merged with the Banco La Guaire CA to form the Banco La Guaira Internacional CA in which BOLAM held a large miniority interest.

In 1964 Barclays Bank DCO, which was already established in the Caribbean joined BOLAM and became its third equal partner. BOLAM continued to do well and by 1970 its offices had grown from 13 to 55 in 10 countries. It was now time for the partnership to be altered and an agreement was reached in 1970 whereby BOLAM, with its branches on the mainland of Latin America, would become a wholly-owned subsidiary of BOLSA. The other two partners would acquire a corresponding shareholding in BOLSA.

Lloyds Bank Europe

In 1911 a subsidiary, or auxiliary company as it was called in those days, was formed abroad when Lloyds acquired Armstrong & Co with branches in Paris and Le Havre for approximately £40,000. The bank was renamed Lloyds Bank (France) Ltd. In 1917 a partnership on a fifty-fifty basis was formed with National Provincial Bank and the name of the auxiliary was changed to Lloyds Bank (France), and National Provincial Bank (France), Ltd. In 1919 the title changed to Lloyds and National Provincial Foreign Bank Ltd. By 1934 it had a branch in the Haymarket and several branches abroad in Belgium, France and Switzerland. Its head office was at 34 Threadneedle Street, London.

The business of the bank was mainly with British companies operating abroad and British expatriates. Most of the branches in the 1920s made large profits only on exchange dealings. The Monte Carlo branch made money from the casino business and Geneva increased their profits from the dollar and sterling balances received from the League of Nations which were lent out to other banks. By 1938, 15 branches were open and deposits totalled £12m. In 1954 National Provincial's holding was purchased. The bank becoming a wholly-owned subsidiary of Lloyds with the name being changed on 3 January 1955 to Lloyds Bank (Foreign) Ltd. The bank's management was improved during the following years. The General Manager, M. H. Finlinson, wrote in 1961: 'On the Continent we now have a first-class management team, average age 48, keen and energetic'. The name of the bank was changed again in 1964 to Lloyds Bank Europe Ltd.

During the 1960s a period of rapid growth occurred helped by the development of the Euro-currency market and wholesale banking. The bank was transformed from a small deposit bank operating in four countries to a major international bank. By 1970 there were 19 branches in Europe. In 1971 the bank was merged with BOLSA to form Lloyds and Bolsa International Bank in which Lloyds held a 51 per cent share. In 1973 this bank became a wholly-owned subsidiary and its name was changed to Lloyds Bank International in 1974.

Above, the old banking hall at Lloyds Bank (Belgium) SA/NV, Meir 52, Antwerp, 12 July 1957. The £10 notice (centre) advises travellers they are allowed to take into or bring out of the United Kingdom up to 10 pounds in sterling notes – but no more! The new banking hall at Teniersbuilding, Antwerp is pictured below. Note the clean lines, flower display and absence of anti-bandit screens at the new building.

Lloyds Bank (Foreign) Ltd, Monte Carlo, about 1960. The branch first opened in 1924 as a sub-agency under the control of the Nice Office. The first branch manager was Hennesy Cook and the title of the bank was Lloyds and National Provincial Foreign Bank Ltd until it changed in 1955 to Lloyds Bank (Foreign) Ltd. There was discussion in 1924 at a Board Meeting in London whether the Bank should open an office in the Casino but this 'was considered to be undesirable'.

Lugano

In 1974 Lloyds Bank International lost over £30 million on unauthorised currency dealing in Lugano, Switzerland. The Lugano branch was set up about 1968 and was the smallest of the bank's three Swiss branches. The events leading up to this are told in the book *Great Financial Disasters* published by Arthur Barker Limited. This is a humorous book and a certain amount of poetic licence may have been taken by the author, Alex Murray, in the following account:

'Towards the end of 1972 Marc Colombo, a 26 year-old Swiss who had worked for Midland Bank as a currency dealer, was offered a job in the small branch of Lloyds Bank International in the Swiss town of Lugano, near the Italian border. He was hired at a salary equivalent to £760 per month, and was told by the branch manager Egidio Mombelli that he could expect to earn five or ten times his salary in profits on dealing in currencies. Dealing? Or gambling? Colombo's view of his job was straightforward. "A foreign exchange dealer is by definition a speculator. It is a gambler's profession." It was some while before his employers learnt of his philosophy – but they learnt alright.

Colombo started enthusiastically, and before long was making a good return for the bank in this most volatile and fast-moving of international markets, in which huge sums are transferred by banks' dealers around the world in seconds, and currency values shift on the slightest rumours or news stories.

In February 1973 Mombelli, some 12 years older than Colombo, was impressed by the work of the young dealer and made him head of the foreign exchange operation at the branch, which employed 16 people altogether. Lugano may be smaller than Zurich and Geneva but it is large enough for a number of thriving bank branches. For Lloyds, based in London, international currency dealing in its five-year-old Lugano branch was regulated by a three-volume book of rules, which was constantly being updated. There were also occasional visits by head office staff, and the Swiss authorities themselves required regular reports on bank business. But this Swiss-Italian branch of an English clearing bank seemed to be doing well, Mombelli was pleased, Lloyds was pleased – and young Marc was especially pleased.

In October 1973 the Egyptians launched their offensive against Israel in the Yom Kippur War, whose effect on international markets promised to be vast. Colombo, in the traditional manner of foreign exchange dealers keen to make money on the slightest turn in the market, took the view that the dollar, the world's main currency, would weaken as a result of the conflict. In November, he sold $34 million of the American currency in the "forward" market, i.e. he contracted to deliver this amount of dollars in three month's time, hoping that the rate would then be lower, so that he could buy these dollars cheaply on the "spot" (or day-to-day) market and make a good profit when he delivered them. Unfortunately, 1973 was also the year of the trebling of oil prices and the energy crisis, which started to push the dollar up in the world's markets rather than weaken it.

Things were going wrong.

In January 1974 Colombo reckoned his position was looking so desperate that he would have to buy in the dollars he needed before the currency rose any further. He took an overall loss of seven million Swiss francs. It was an enormous figure, considering that the daily "open" limit of the branch was not supposed to be more than five million Swiss francs. He was obviously facing severe retribution, perhaps the sack, if he brought this to the notice of the management, as he was supposed to do, so he decided to make back the money he had lost by doubling up. This time, however, he believed the dollar would rise, as it had been doing consistently. He decided to buy for forward delivery $100 million, of which half he paid for in German marks and the rest in Swiss francs. What happened? You guessed it. The market now took the opposite tack – the dollar started to slide. By March, Colombo was sitting on overall losses of around 50 million Swiss francs.

"I had three choices", he said later. One was to admit his mistakes, another was to hold firm and hope for a turn in the market, and the third was to reverse the position, hoping for a drop in the dollar. No need to guess which way he jumped. "I chose the last possibility", he said. "I was at all times convinced I could recoup the losses. But I felt I was a prisoner of events."

He decided to sell the extraordinary sum of $592 million forward, betting that the dollar would fall, and massive profits would more than wipe out the losses. But once again he got it wrong. The dollar rose steadily in value. By now, he was dealing in many positions day by day, vastly exceeding the limits imposed by Lloyds.

In August, someone in Lloyds in London overheard a telephone conversation indicating that there were some massive forward deals with the Lugano branch. Officials flew out. They discovered that at that very moment the "open" position of the branch was a staggering $592 million sold, 844 million Deutschmarks bought, and six million French francs bought. The bank's official limit for open positions at the branch was the equivalent of five million Swiss francs; and the actual recorded position of the branch at that time was less than a million dollars. Colombo and Mombelli were suspended. In a terse press statement in London, Lloyds disclosed that the branch had taken a loss equivalent to £33 million on the unauthorised deals.

The full extent of the operations by Colombo came to light in a four-day court case in Switzerland in which Colombo was given an eighteen-month suspended sentence for violating Swiss banking law and falsifying documents, and Mombelli received a six-month suspended sentence for banking irregularities. It appeared that Colombo had been financing these huge foreign exchange positions by borrowing money from a range of Swiss banking institution in Lloyds' name, and entering them as currency deals in the branch books. Mombelli had said he simply did not notice this, as he was far too busy with other aspects of branch business, and knew little about the foreign exchange market. "For every dealer you need at least four administrators to check what he is doing. They do things that no ordinary banker understands," he said.

Lloyds' own rules were tightened up after that, as were those in many international banks. There had never been an allegation that Colombo was dealing for personal profit, merely that he had used his employer's money to behave as if he was in a casino. "I knew there were two or three copies of the book of rules around the office, but nobody paid any attention to it", Colombo commented.'

Bank Chairmen, Directors and General Managers

The collapse of a large private bank in Birmingham and the passing of new legislation which allowed banks to limit their shareholders' liability persuaded Lloyds that they needed to improve their capital base. Consequently in 1865 they merged with the local bank Moilliet and Sons and became a joint stock company under the title of Lloyds Banking Company Limited. The new Company had an authorised capital of £2 million, seven offices, a staff of 50 and 4,524 accounts.

Timothy Kenrick

Timothy Kenrick, born in 1807, was the first Chairman of Lloyds Banking Company. He became Chairman in 1865, when he was 58. Kenrick had no banking experience, though he had married into the family of the Leicestershire bankers, Paget and Co. He started his business career in the family iron-foundry and hardware manufacturing business. He was an active and generous supporter of the local Education League and the General Hospital. He was also practically the founder of the Nurse's Training Institute. In 1858 he became a Director of the Midland Railway Company and later became a Deputy Chairman. Upon becoming Chairman of the Bank he proved he was more than just a figurehead by engaging in negotiations with a correspondent about the discounting of bills.

Sampson S. Lloyd

Sampson Samuel Lloyd was Chairman from 1868 to 1886. He became Chairman of Lloyds Bank at the early age of 48 and was a descendant of Sampson Lloyd II, an original partner of the Birmingham bank. He entered the Bank at the age of 19 and was made a partner in 1843 when he was 23. When the Bank became a joint stock bank he became Managing Director. He later resigned in 1868 in order to enter political life but the same year rejoined the Bank as Chairman. He continued with his political activities and was eventually elected as Conservative Member of Parliament for Plymouth in 1874. He remained an MP for only one Parliamentary session.

Sampson Lloyd made his banking name with his participation in a scheme for a country clearing system. He along with F. Bassett and Theodore Harris of Leighton Buzzard, W. Gillett of Banbury, O. Heywood of Manchester and W. C. Tunstall of the Gloucestershire Banking Company planned to establish in London a separate Country Clearing House. However, the plan was superseded by a scheme devised by Sir John Lubbock when the Country Clearing was established in 1858 as part of the existing London Bankers' Clearing House.

In 1884 Lloyds Banking Company merged with two London Banks, Bosanquet Salt and Co and Barnetts, Hoares, Hanbury and Lloyd. The new bank was called Lloyds, Barnetts and Bosanquets Bank Ltd. The head office remained in Birmingham although London was becoming more and more important. In 1886 Thomas Salt became the third Chairman.

Thomas Salt

He was born in 1830 and was educated at Rugby, where he won the English Essay Prize, and at Balliol College, Oxford, he gained a first in law and history. After graduating from Oxford he entered the family banking business of Stevenson, Salt and Webb. In 1859 he represented Stafford as their Conservative MP. In 1865 he withdrew from politics to give greater attention to the banking firm. In 1866 the Staffordshire banking firm was sold to Lloyds Banking Company with Thomas Salt joining the Board of Directors. The London bank of Bosanquet Salt and Co in Lombard Street continued with Thomas Salt as partner. In 1869 Salt re-entered Parliament and in 1880 held a junior office in Disraeli's Government. He also became Chairman of the North Staffordshire Railway and of the New Zealand Railway Company. He was also a County Alderman, Chairman of the Lunacy Commission, an Ecclesiastical Commissioner and Public Works Loan Commissioner.

Despite all these activities Salt was still able to attend to his banking duties and he succeeded Sampson Lloyd as Chairman in 1886. The Bank soon changed its title to Lloyds Bank Limited and with Thomas Salt as Chairman and Howard Lloyd as General Manager the Bank started to grow at an enormous rate by absorption of some of the old private banks. During Salt's twelve years in office fifteen banking companies were absorbed with result that the Banks' branches grew from 61 in 1886 to 257 in 1898.

John Spencer Phillips

John Spencer Phillips was the son of a rector from Ludlow. He was educated at Shrewsbury School and Trinity, Cambridge. Upon graduating from Cambridge he joined the Shrewsbury and Welshpool Old Bank which was the banking house of Beck and Co and became a partner. In 1880 the banking business was sold to Lloyds with the result that Spencer Phillips was given a seat on the Board. In 1888 he succeeded Edward Brodie Hoare as Deputy Chairman and in 1898 became Chairman. He was also President of the Institute of Bankers.

Spencer Phillips took a leading part in the many amalgamations that occurred during his term as Chairman. In 1889 Lloyds amalgamated with the Birmingham Joint Stock Bank. This bank which had at one time been Lloyds 'powerful opponent and competitor' in Birmingham was now in poor health.

At the annual general meetings of the Bank, Spencer Phillips left his mark by giving an appraisal of the economic affairs of the nation. He went into long reviews, referring for example, to the economic effects of the Boer War. He also constantly urged that all banks should publish frequent statements of accounts based on averages believing this would settle the question of the supposed insufficiency of London's gold reserves. Previous chairmen had made only brief references to the current economic situation.

Richard Vassar Vassar-Smith

Richard Vassar Vassar-Smith was born in 1843 and educated at King's School, Gloucester. When he left school he joined his father's business of general carriers and agents for the Great Western Railway. In 1870 he became head of the family firm. He went on to become Chairman of the Port Talbot Steel Co, the Gloucester Railway Carriage and Wagon Co and the Gloucester Gas Light Company. In 1886 he became

Mayor of Gloucester for the year. He was also a Director of the Worcester Bank and when Lloyds Bank absorbed the Worcester City & County Bank in 1889 he was invited to join the Board of the Bank. In 1909 he succeeded Spencer Phillips as Chairman when Lloyds Bank was one of the largest banks in the country.

During his term in office he was engaged in discussions with the authorities regarding wartime arrangements. In recognition of this service he was created a baronet in 1917. He had many outside interests and was a strong churchman and a freemason. In 1917/18 he was President of the Federation of British Industries. He declined several invitations to stand as a Conservative candidate for election to Parliament. He took a great interest in sport and the outside activities of the bank staff. When he died, still in office in 1922, the staff felt that they had lost a great chairman. A collection was started which raised £10,000 for a memorial in the form of a benevolent fund for the bank staff and their dependants. The Vassar-Smith Fund still continues today supported entirely by voluntary contributions and administered by Lloyds Bank Group Staff Union, but eligibility to benefit is open to all Bank Staff, whether union members or not.

Lord Wardington

J. W. Beaumont Pease succeeded Vassar-Smith as Chairman in 1922. He had been Deputy Chairman throughout his chairmanship. Through his mother, Helen Maria Fox, Beaumont Pease was directly descended from Sampson Lloyd II who was one of the four founding partners of Taylors and Lloyds. He was educated at Oxford and joined the banking firm of Hodgkin, Barnett, Pease, Spense and Co of Newcastle upon Tyne. In 1903 when this old banking partnership was absorbed by Lloyds, Beaumont Pease was offered a seat on the board.

He remained Chairman for 23 years until 1945 and served four terms as Chairman of the Committee of London Clearing Bankers and President of the British Bankers' Association. During his term in office the Bank acquired a reputation for caution. He was the symbol of honesty and integrity and a first class after-dinner speaker. He was also a considerable sportsman. He became Lord Wardington of Alnmouth in the County of Northumberland in 1936.

Lord Balfour of Burleigh

Balfour of Burleigh started his career in the city as a clerk in the Alliance Assurance Co in 1907. During the early part of World War I he was an interpreter and in 1915 he transferred to the Intelligence Branch. After the war he continued with his career and by 1938 he had risen to become Chairman of The National Bank of New Zealand. He was also a director of other banks and institutions and when in January 1946 he became Chairman of the Bank he resigned his directorship of the District Bank.

He was an aristocrat from an old Scottish family and played his part in public affairs through his position as a Scottish representative peer in the House of Lords. He made his first speech on 24 April 1923.

During Balfour's term in office one of his special concerns was to change the Bank's training methods which had not changed for years. He became a popular chairman. Upon his retirement in 1954 the staff subscribed to buy him a Ford Consul convertible. Staff were asked to contribute up to a maximum of 1s (5p) each. After his death in 1967, the car was lent by Lady Balfour to the motor museum at Beaulieu.

Sir Richard Vassar Vassar-Smith, 1843–1922. Chairman, 1909–1922. From the painting by Sir William Orpen, RA.

J. W. Beaumont Pease, later Lord Wardington, 1869–1950. Chairman, 1922–1945.

The Right Hon Lord Balfour of Burleigh, 1883–1967. Chairman, 1946–1954. From the painting by James Gunn, ARA.

The Right Hon Lord Franks of Headington. Chairman, 1954–1962. From the painting by William Dring, RA.

Lord Franks of Headington

Sir Oliver (later Lord) Franks became Chairman in November 1954. Unlike most of his predecessors he did not have any banking connections but was a pre-war don. During the war he was a civil servant. The head of an Oxford College and ex-ambassador, he had a brilliant intellect and distinguished himself with his lively mind and tremendous ability. He got on well with the general management of the bank. He advocated that the Bank should take on more graduates but was unable to make much progress. A senior official of the Bank wrote in 1957 of his firm belief that the majority of the executive positions in the future would not be held by graduates and was greatly opposed to any policy of introducing special terms to entice their recruitment. During Sir Oliver's time as Chairman there still existed the restrictive environment and cautious attitudes of all the major clearing banks.

Sir Harald Peake

Harald Peake succeeded as Chairman in February 1962. He had been a Director since 1941 and a Vice-Chairman since 1947. He was not a trained banker having come from a Yorkshire coal-mine-owning family. He was Chairman of the Steel Company of Wales from 1955 to 1962 and was a Director of Rolls Royce and a number of other companies. During the war he had been Director of Public Relations in the RAF, 1940–42, and Director of Air Force Welfare, 1942/43. His main objective as Chairman was to improve communications with shareholders and staff. He involved himself with major issues and was one of the prime movers for the attempted merger of the Bank with Barclays and Martins in 1968.

Sir Eric Faulkner

In February 1969, Eric Faulkner succeeded Harald Peake as Chairman. He was educated at Bradfield College and Corpus Christi College, Cambridge. His banking career began at Glyn Mills and Co in 1936. After war service he rejoined Glyn Mills and Co in 1946 and went on to become an Executive Director in 1950 and was their Chairman between 1963 and 1968. When he took the chair he had spent 32 years in banking and had also an extensive knowledge of industry. During his eight years in office in Lloyds his dynamism and professionalism raised the status of the Bank in this country and abroad.

Sir Jeremy Morse

Sir Jeremy became Chairman in 1977. His family were brewers in East Anglia and he was educated at Winchester College and graduated from New College, Oxford. After National Service he joined Glyn Mills & Co as a trainee. Here he worked with hand written ledgers and learned the skill of casting. After three years as a trainee and subsequent spells with the stockbroking firm of Cazenove and Co, and chartered accountants and auditors Cooper Brothers and Co, he became a local director of Glyn Mills.

In 1964 Glyn Mills sent him on a tour of the USA in the company of senior Scottish investment trust managers. Upon his return he was invited by the Bank of England to join them as an Executive Director. In May 1975 Sir Jeremy became Deputy Chairman of Lloyds Bank and Chairman two years later.

Sir Harald Peake, 1899–1978. Chairman, 1962–1969. From the painting by Edward I. Halliday.

Mr E. O. Faulkner pictured when Chairman-Elect of Lloyds Bank.

Sir Eric Faulkner and the present Chairman, Sir Jeremy Morse, after the 'handover' at the AGM 31 March 1977.

Directors of the Birmingham Joint Stock Bank. This bank was established in 1861 and was absorbed by Lloyds Bank in 1889, who thus acquired the bank which had been their 'powerful opponent and competitor' in Birmingham.

The Board of Directors of Lloyds Bank, 15 December 1978. Seated from left to right: C. J. Montgomery, CBE; Sir Michael Wilson, MBE; Sir Michael Clapham, KBE, LLD; Sir Reginald Verdon-Smith, LLD, DL; Sir Jeremy Morse, KCMG (Chairman); N. W. Jones, TD; A. J. Davis, RD; Sir Eric Faulkner, MBE; Sir Ivor Baker, CBE, DL; George M. Williams, CBE, MC, TD, DL; The Right Hon The Earl of Morley; Sir Bernard Scott, CBE, TD, LLD; The Right Hon Lord Lloyd, MBE, DL; G. C. Kent; The Right Hon Viscount Caldecote, DSC; Sir Daniel Pettit; Roland A. Cookson, CBE, DCL; R. O. Steel; The Right Hon Viscount Bearsted, TD, DL; Sir Patrick Hamilton, Bt; Sir Lindsay Alexander, The Most Hon The Marquess of Abergavenny, KG, OBE; A. B. Hampton, TD, DL; S. James L. Hill, DSO, MC; Sir Arnold Hall, FRS; The Right Hon Lord Kenyon, CBE, LLD, DL; Sir Peter Matthews; The Right Hon Lord Aldington, PC, KCMG, CBE, DSO, TD, DL. Seated on the left: D. H. Davies (Secretary).

The first meeting of Directors after the merger of Lloyds Bank Plc with Lloyds Bank International, January 1986. Pictured are: Michael Thompson, George Duncan, John Davis, Viscount Caldecote, Alastair Michie (Secretary), Sir Jeremy Morse, Brian Pitman, Eric Whittle, Eric Swainson, Russell Smith, Sir Peter Ramsbotham, Norman Jones, John Raisman, Sir Henry Plumb, Sir Alec Merrison, Sir Peter Matthews, Geoffrey Kent, Sir George Jefferson, Sir Lindsay Alexander, Fred Crawley, Sir Robin Ibbs, Sir Gordon Hobday, Sir John Hedley Greenborough and Lord Hanson.

Regional General Managers meeting, 1950s. Pictured are Messrs Fall, Fagan, Whittaker, Ensor, Hill, Hynwood, Faux and Warburton.

Joint General Managers meeting, 1956. Pictured are Messrs Guyer, Faux, Boyes, Hill, Warburton, Lawson, Andrews and Woolley.

Bank Directors, fortnightly meeting, 1950s. Some of the people pictured include: Lord Hutchison, Sir Alexander R. Murray, Lord Wardington, Sir Jeremy Raisman, Harald Peake, Lord Balfour of Burleigh, E. Whitley-Jones, A. H. Ensor, L. D. Williams, Sir Peter Bennet, Lt.-Col. R. K. Morcom.

Annual Planning Conference, Kingswood Staff College, 6–8 April 1979, attended by Chief Executives to discuss, in depth, plans crucial to the future of the Bank. Those who attended were: Trust Division General Manager, F. H. Freeman; General Manager (Group Finance), J. B. Rees; G. B. Hague (General Manager, Management Service Division); R. J. Medlam; A. D. C. Mckie; C. F. Blewett; Sir Jeremy Morse; General Manager (Overseas), D. W. Kendrick; Head of Corporate Planning, E. J. Dawson; Joint General Manager, G. C. Evans; Deputy Chief General Manager, F. W. Crawley; Corporate Planning Manager, R. A. Wakefield; Joint General Manager, G. R. Turner; General Manager (Staff and Administration), T. F. H. Cullum; Assistant Chief General Managers, T. J. Howes and R. R. Amos; Chief General Manager, A. J. Davis; and C. L. McL Johnson, the Bank's Economic Adviser.

Blists Hill Open Air Museum

In May 1987 a replica of Lloyds Bank's Broseley branch, as it looked in the late 19th century, was opened at the Blists Hill Open Air Museum in Shropshire which is part of the Ironbridge Gorge Museum Trust's complex. The building is modelled on the present Lloyds Bank sub-branch at Broseley. This particular bank was probably built by Pritchard, Gordon and Co, local private bankers, shortly before their takeover by Lloyds in 1888.

The replica building was sponsored and largely furnished by Lloyds Bank. The counters were constructed within the museum, mainly from the original fittings of Grey Street, Newcastle branch and from another branch at Stonehouse, Plymouth, which had been closed down. The small items were assembled from branches throughout the country with as many as possible deriving from the West Midlands.

Visitors to the Blists Hill Open Air Museum (which is a living museum of a community in the year 1895) can exchange their decimal currency at the bank for tokens. These tokens are in denominations of a farthing, halfpenny, penny and threepence and can be spent in the shops situated in the museum.

Museum potter outside the bank having deposited his days takings. Note the cast iron letters BANK above the manager's office. Apart from the City of London, hanging signs were not widely introduced until the late 1920s.

Bank teller, Ted Stuart, In Victorian costume, counting tokens which can be spent in the museum.

In the 1890s there were no bank statements as we know them today. The wealthier customers had their own ledger-books, similar to that shown above. Most customers, however, used passbooks, which were sent to the branch periodically to be brought up to date. The entries would be entered in a copperplate hand and sent back to the customer for his agreement. Statements, as we know them, were not common until after the Second World War.

Manager's office. A branch the size of Broseley would have had a manager and two or three clerks. The branch manager would have been paid at least £200 per annum.

The manager had the luxury of a gas fire.

Clerk's desk. A first clerk would have been paid around £150 per annum while a probationer or junior would have received between £25–£50 per annum.

Pewter inkwell. Erasures were not allowed in bank books – entries had to be run through with a pen.

Cashier's box made of oak, on permanent loan to the Museum from a Taunton branch customer.

Gladstone coin bag with a handle on the end for dragging the money along the ground.

Lloyds Bank clock.

Calendar and gas light. Working conditions were bad in winter, with inadequate light for ledger work.

Coin scoop.

Weight which served for £5 of silver or for 5s of copper. Since decimalisation things have become more complicated. We now have weights for £20 of one pound coins, £10 of fifty penny pieces, £10 of twenty penny pieces, £5 of silver and finally £1 and 50p of bronze.

Beamscales. When the lever is released, the brass pans rest, reducing the pressure on the end knife-edges.

Letter balance.

Chubb safe.

Leather fire-bucket filled with sand. Note the initials LBL.

Lloyds Bank mahogany chair with leather upholstery, used by customers.

Cashier's wooden stool.

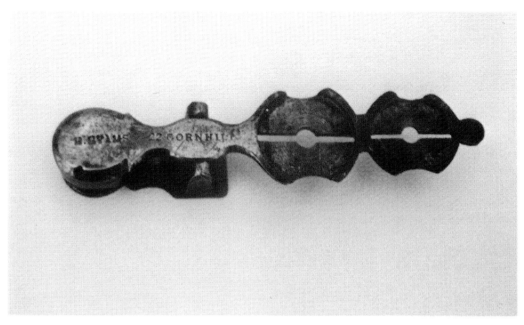

Brass seasaw balance used for weighing sovereigns and half-sovereigns. These scales had slots to gauge the sizes of the two coins. Coin scales declined in use after 1917 when gold coins were taken out of the currency.

Watch stand.

Gold changer machine formerly owned by a customer of Bath C & C branch.

Cox & Co

In February 1923, Cox & Co, was taken over by Lloyds Bank. The takeover was suggested by the Bank of England as Cox & Co were in financial difficulties and a run on the bank was expected any day. The Bank of England had to give Lloyds two guarantees totalling £900,000 before they would announce the acquisition.

Cox & Co were West End bankers to the Army with branches in Burma, Egypt and India. The history of this bank started in 1758 when Richard Cox was appointed Colonel's Clerk or agent, in order to keep the accounts of the First Foot Guards (The Grenadier Guards). The Colonel's Clerk was a civilian attached to each regiment who received the annual payments voted by Parliament. Their job was to set aside money for troops' clothing and compulsory subscriptions to the Chelsea Hospital (or 'off-reckonings') and to distribute the rest as pay to officers and men. The clerk's commission was twopence in each pound. Within ten years Cox had added the Royal Artillery and ten other regiments to the books of what had now become Cox & Co. Expansion of the business meant successive changes of premises, from Albemarle Street to Craig's Court in the 1760s, from Craig's Court to Charing Cross in 1888 and finally to Pall Mall in 1923. To cope with the new class of business arising from their Eastern branches Cox & Co opened an office in Gracechurch Street in 1922. It is interesting to note that the officers of the Guards had the privilege of going to a special counter where they could call for the ledger in order to inspect their accounts.

In 1914 Cox's (as Army men called it) had a staff of 180 which by 1918 had risen to 4,500. Through the 1914–18 War the office was manned day and night with cheques being cashed 24 hours a day, Sundays and Bank Holidays included, for the officers arriving from or returning to the front. The bank never closed its doors.

Cox & Co had a rival, across the road in Pall Mall and in the City namely the bank of Henry S. King & Co which was founded in 1816. This small family firm had a long history as booksellers, stationers, East India agents, shippers and bankers. From 1868 the business concentrated on banking and agency work in connection with Indian trade. It had an office in Cornhill and a branch in India. In 1922 the ageing senior partner, with no successor in sight, arranged an amalgamation with Cox & Co. The new bank which was created, 'Cox's & King's', was almost immediately taken over by Lloyds Bank. By that time the company had offices all along the old sea routes to India and in the sub-continent itself. Its traditional army business had expanded rapidly to include the Indian Army, the Indian Civil Service and the British Army in India. The name is still remembered in the flourishing travel agency of Cox & Kings.

In 1960 the banking business in the Indian sub-continent became the subject of a transaction between Lloyds and National and Grindlays Bank, whereby Grindlays acquired the Lloyds Eastern branches in return for a 25 per cent stake in Grindlays Bank.

The following pictures were taken about 1919 prior to the amalgamations, when Cox & Co were at 16 Charing Cross. Note the number of women employed. No women were employed as clerks until the 1914–18 War. However, there is some evidence that they were involved in non-clerical work as telephonists from the beginning of this century. The new recruits quickly adapted to banking work. Many of the men who were demobilised in 1919 had no civilian clothes so they had to wear their army uniforms in the bank while their suits were being made.

Joint General Managers.

Correspondence Section.

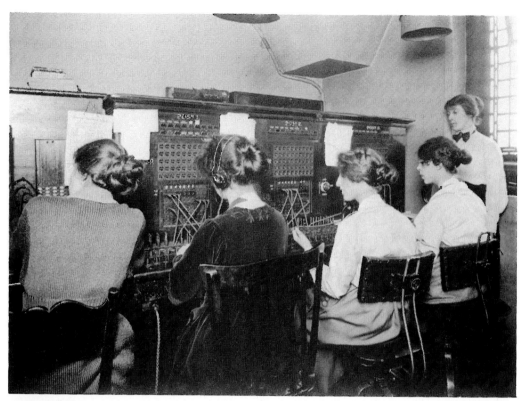

Telephonists.

'Staff' Pay Department. In Cox & Co's rule book (1916) it was stated that male members of staff were to converse with lady members only on matters of business.

Typing Section. The first typewriters were made commercially in the USA in 1873 by Remingtons — the gunsmith.

Ledger Room. All the book-keeping was done by hand and accounts kept in ledgers. Copies of the accounts were written in copperplate into passbooks.

Demobilisation and Gratuity Department.

Demobilisation and Gratuity Department, Filing Room.

Girl Guides acting as messengers during the 1914–18 War.

Cashiers, Foreign and Commercial Branch. Note the open mahogany counter.

Second World War

The following extract is from the booklet *Lloyds Bank Limited, Executor and Trustee Department, 1939–1947*:

'1939 – RUMOURS OF WAR – and the Executor and Trustee Department, like other business houses, took steps to protect its personnel and records. Important documents were copied and sent to country towns, ARP instructions given, underground safes strengthened as shelters and plans made to transfer at short notice the Chief Office Staff and a great accumulation of records from Threadneedle Street, London, to Ewhurst Place in the heart of the Surrey countryside. There were naturally mixed feelings about evacuation. To the younger members of Staff, without family responsibilities, it was a novel adventure, but the cautious asked what young typists' parents would think – and then, of course, what were wives going to say!

On the 29th of August it was decided to leave London literally overnight. Seven large removal vans were hired and packed and the Staff, apart from those going with the vans, were given sketch maps and told to make their way to Ewhurst the next day with sufficient clothing for a week or two. Most of the "week-end" cases, however, were not finally brought back for nearly eight years.

The convoy of lorries set off when it was dark – after an impressive ceremony at which sandwiches and bottles of beer were distributed with a hearty "Good Luck" from a Head Office official. After such a send-off anything might be expected.

The lorries eventually reached Ewhurst at two o'clock in the morning. Numerous further journeys were made during the following days to fetch more of the contents of the London office, only sufficient being left for the skeleton Staff who remained and underwent all the rigours and inconvenience to which the City was subjected.'

German troops outside Lloyds Bank, Alderney branch, during the Second World War. German forces occupied the Channel Islands on Sunday, 30 June 1940. Communications with Head Office then ceased. A special department was set up in Head Office to reconstruct the accounts of the Channel Islands branches. This was possible because every branch had a custodian branch where duplicate records were kept of all the transactions. Once the accounts were reconstructed in London, business was conducted on normal lines.

Coventry Blitz, 14 November 1940. National Provincial Bank can be seen centre and Lloyds Bank, with the damaged roof, is to the left. During the war 641 branches were damaged but only 32 branches out of a total of approximately 2,000 were destroyed. In only two cases of the branches destroyed did this include the strong rooms.

Monument branch (left), after being hit by German bombs during the Blitz. The branch was gutted and many others were severely damaged. The ordinary banking branches in London stayed open during the war unlike specialised departments like Clearing Department which moved to Stoke-on-Trent.

Branches

The banks in Wales can be traced back to the drovers, who would travel from fair to fair in the early summer buying up the hardy Welsh Black Cattle. The herd would then be driven to Essex and Kent where the cattle were rested and fattened up for the Michaelmas markets. At these markets the drovers would exchange the cattle for gold.

Some drovers also acted as agents for the Government taking Welsh Ship Money collected by agents of Charles I to London. On their trip they sometimes carried the rents collected by the stewards of Welsh estates to their landlords in England. The money-carrying drovers attracted the highwaymen and gangs of footpads. In order to survive the drovers needed a banking system.

It was David Jones, the son of a farmer and associated with droving, who brought a simple, rural banking system to Wales. At the age of 15, David was working at the *King's Head* at Llandovery. The inn was on the droving route and a regular stopover for the drovers. Often David was asked to look after their money for them while they were staying at the inn. This gave him the idea of starting a bank.

David Jones married well and with his bride's money and his savings he started the Banc yr Eidion Du in 1799. In order to inspire confidence in his bank with reluctant farmers who did not like parting with their gold in exchange for a piece of paper he hit upon a reassuring idea. In the left-hand corner of his banknotes he had engraved the outline of the Welsh Black Ox, which was an emblem showing the close association between banking and farming.

The bank prospered and on his death passed to his three grandsons. The business stayed in the family until 1909 when it was sold to Lloyds Bank. The bank in Llandovery is still in the same building, Prospect House, High Street, where the family moved in 1903. This imposing building has red sandstone pillars and fluted over the portal are the founder's initials. It is interesting to note that until the outbreak of war in 1939, the bank continued to issue cheques marked with the Black Ox. Many customers to this very day still call the Llandovery branch, Banc Yr Eidion Du.

Research has shown that the burial site of Nipper, the HMV dog, is a corner in the car park behind the Bank's branch in Clarence Street, Kingston Upon Thames, Surrey. The car park was originally a private garden. Francis Barraud was responsible for the original painting of Nipper sitting by a gramophone and the model used was his brother's dog, a half-breed fox terrier. Mr Barraud managed to get the Gramophone Company interested in buying the painting and copyright for the sum of £100 in 1899. In Britain, 'The Gramophone Company', later 'The Gramophone and Typewriter Limited', registered the dog minus its title in 1900. It was not until about 1912 that the words 'His Master's Voice' were added and this then became the official trademark.

REGD. TRADE MARK OF THE GRAMOPHONE CO. LTD

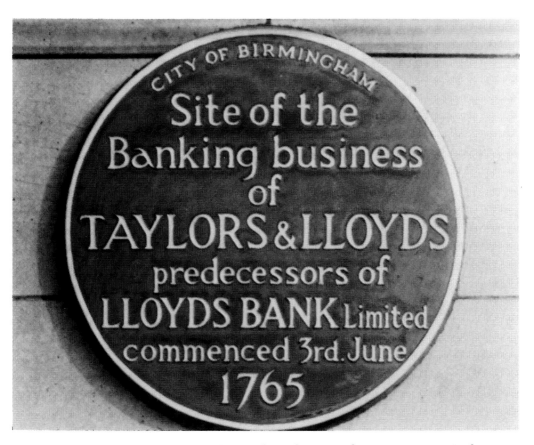

Taylors and Lloyds, started their bank at Dale End, Birmingham in June 1765. They were paying interest at 2 per cent for deposits from September 1765. By 1775 they had 277 customers on their books, consisting mostly of traders and small manufacturers.

Fareham branch of the Hampshire Banking Company, 1867. This bank later became part of the Capital and Counties Bank before its amalgamation with Lloyds Bank in 1918.

ROBBERY

OF THE

ASHFORD BANK.

On **TUESDAY** the 12th **DECEMBER** 1826, between One and half-past One o'clock, whilst the Clerk was gone to Dinner, the Cash Drawers were removed to the Deposit which with the inner and outer Doors of the Bank were left locked and otherwise secured as usual, when the following Notes were **STOLEN**, the Payment of which is stopped.

Ashford Bank £5.

2045	2708	3023	3593
2049	2720	3044	3640
2050	2727	3056	3664
2052	2728	3080	3703
2079	2738	3095	3780
2163	2743	3111	3795
2192	2752	3120	3814
2209	2782	3171	3819
2217	2791	3174	3831
2243	2793	3187	3861
2270	2802	3228	3886
2278	2815	3247	3903
2292	2818	3255	3981
2326	2850	3473	3999
2363	2854	3981	4000
2378	2862	3283	4016
2391	2871	3294	4070
2400	2887	3297	4083
2403	2888	3303	4203
2462	2899	3344	4250
2480	2909	3346	4263
2491	2930	3367	4279
2543	2950	3374	4286
2607	2977	3412	4404
2623	2992	3416	4635
2647	3005	3480	
2678	3010	3526	

Ashford Bank £10.

1002	1332	1572	1782
1005	1343	1589	1787
1039	1347	1602	1800
1033	1355	1608	1801
1051	1356	1617	1807
1054	1365	1632	1632
1075	1381	1650	1836
1078	1402	1672	1840
1089	1415	1685	1847
1104	1428	1696	1849
1107	1433	1716	1859
1124	1450	1718	1861
1140	1453	1720	1883
1141	1461	1721	1884
1157	1473	1725	1921
1107	1485	1727	1935
1221	1501	1735	1946
1239	1505	1745	1962
1240	1511	1747	1967
1261	1528	1751	1973
1268	1553	1753	1999
1276	1568	1778	
1281	1056	1486	

Bank of England £10.
7349 7350 7351 Dated Feb. 11, 1826

Canterbury.
1006, 1172.

Rye, 2521.   *Dover* 915.

Canterbury Union 493, 709, 1196
1257, 1349, 1488.

Ashford Commercial 942.

Canterbury 339. **£20.**

Canterbury **£5.**
67, 293, 449, 569, 839 1034 1140, 1324,
1359 1457, 1675, 1710, 2298, 3059,
3561, 3679.

Rye, 1842.

Dover 107, 161, 667, 789, 819, 927, 1067, 1035, 1292, 1322, 1344, 1426, 1487, 1555, 2449, 3088. *Kentish* 5697, 8426, 7369, 7819. *Faversham* 3593, 4407, 4643

Canterbury Union 993, 1222, 1234, 1357, 1418, 1634, 1656, 1828, 2064, 2067, 2198, 2369, 2475, 2493, 2606, 2987, 3334, 3340, 4018.

Cranbrook 56, 116, 1149, 2451, 2535, 2022, 2083.

Sandwich 8892. *Ashford Commercial* 1122.

Bankers and others on receiving Notes are earnestly requested to take notice of and compare the numbers with the above List, and to make particular enquiry of any Persons offering for payment any of the Notes abovementioned, as to their possession thereof, and communicate thereon.

ELLIOTT, PRINTER, ASHFORD.

Truncheon given to Mark Oldershaw when a junior at the Nottingham branch, about 1875. The wooden truncheon is approximately 15 inches long and has leather straps.

Interior of Peacock, Willson & Co, Newark, about 1900. This bank was taken over by Lloyds Bank in 1912. In those days typewriters were not common place and letters had to be written by hand in copying ink. Letters were copied on a hand-press with the aid of dampened blue cloths, which, if made too wet, had the effect of making the ink run so that the letter would become unreadable. This meant that the letter had to be re-written. Copies of confidential letters and information regarding customers were kept in locked books to which only the manager had access.

Oldbury branch, the first branch of Lloyds and Co, established 1864. This picture was taken about 1887 when the Bank was known as Lloyds, Barnetts and Bosanquets Bank Limited. The opening of this branch was the beginning of the rapid growth of a network of Lloyds branches throughout the Midlands. The more recent picture was taken in the 1960s. The exterior has changed little except for the centre doorway being filled in.

PLACES OF BUSINESS.

HEAD OFFICES { LONDON : 71 Lombard Street, E.C.
{ BIRMINGHAM : Edmund Street.

BRANCHES.

LONDON : City Office—72, Lombard Street, E.C.; Colonial & Foreign Department
—60, Lombard Street, E.C.; West End—16, St. James's Street, S.W.; Law
Courts—222, Strand, W.C.; Aldersgate Street, E.C.; Belgrave Road, S.W.;
Cheapside, E.C.; East City—Fenchurch Street; Finchley Road, N.W.; Hampstead—Rosslyn Hill, N.W.; Holborn Circus, E.C.; Knightsbridge—16, Brompton
Road, S.W.; 399 and 401, Oxford Street, W.; Paddington—Cambridge Street, W.;
66, West Smithfield, E.C.; West Kensington—Hammersmith Road, W.

BIRMINGHAM : Colmore Row, High Street, Temple Row, New Street,
Aston Road, Acocks Green, Bearwood, Bloomsbury, Bournville,
Bristol Street, Cape Hill, Deritend, Edgbaston, Erdington, Gooch Street,
Great Hampton Street, Handsworth, Harborne, Highgate, Holyhead Road,
Jamaica Row, King's Norton, Ladywood, Moseley, Parade, Selly Oak,
Small Heath, Sparkbrook, Sparkhill, Stirchley, and Summerfield.

Aberdare	Bracknell	Crediton
Abergavenny	Bradford	Cullompton
Abertillery	Brecon	Darlaston
Allendale Town	Bridgend	Darlington
Alnwick	Bridgnorth	Dartmouth
Altrincham	Bridport	Darwen
Amlwch	Brighton (8 Offices)	Dawlish
Ammanford	Bristol (8 Offices)	Deal
Annfield Plain	Brixham	Derby
Ashbourn	Broadheath	Devonport
Ashburton	Broadstairs	Doncaster
Ashby-de-la-Zouch	Bromsgrove	Dorchester
Ashford	Broseley	Douglas (I. of Man)
Ashington	Buckingham	Dover
Atherstone	Buckley	Dowlais
Avonmouth	Butleigh Salterton	Droitwich
Axminster	Burford (Oxon)	Dudley
Aylesbury	Burslem	Durham
Banbury	Burton-on-Trent	Dursley
Bangor	Caerphilly	Easthourne
Bargoed	Camborne	East Grinstead
Barnstaple	Cambridge	Eastleigh
Barry Dock	Cannock	Ebbw Vale
Bath	Canterbury	Edenbridge
Beaumaris	Cardiff (4 Offices)	Ellesmere
Bellingham	Cardiff Docks	Enfield
Bethesda	Cardigan	Evesham
Bexhill-on-Sea	Carmarthen	Exeter
Bideford	Carnarvon	Exmouth
Birkenhead (3 Offices)	Caterham Valley	Falmouth
Birley (Co.Durham)	Chatham	Furingdon
Bishop Auckland	Cheltenham	Fenton (Staffs.)
Blackhill	Chosham	Fishguard
(Co. Durham)	Chester-le-Street	Fishponds (Bristol)
Blackburn	Chester (4 Offices)	Foleshill
Blackwood	Cinderford	Folkestone
Blaenavon	Cirencester	Forest Hall
Blaydon-upon-Tyne	Clifton (Bristol)	Fowey
Bloxwich	Cliftonville(Margate)	Gateshead
Blyth	Coalville	Gloucester
Bodmin	Coleford	Gosport
Bournemouth	Colehill	Great Bridge
(4 Offices)	Connah's Quay	Halesowen
Bourton-on-the-Water	Corbridge	Hanley
Brackley	Consett	Hastings
	Coventry	Haverfordwest

Hawarden		
Hednesford		
Hemel Hempstead		
Hereford		
Heswall (Cheshire)		
Hexham		
Holsworthy		
Honiton		
Horley		
Hove		
Hull		
Hythe (Kent)		
Ilfracombe		
Iron Bridge		
Jarrow		
Keighley		
Kenilworth		
Kidderminster		
Kingsbridge		
Kingston(Portsmouth)		
Kingswood (Bristol)		
Lampeter		
Landport(Portsmouth)		
Launceston		
Leamington		
Leeds (8 Offices)		
Leicester		
Leominster		
Lichfield		
Liskeard		
Liverpool (10 Offices)		
Llandilo		
Llandudno		
Llandyssul		
Llanelly		
Llanfairfechan		
Longton		
Loughborough		
Ludlow		
Lydney		
Lynton		
Maesteg		
Maidenhead		
Maidstone		
Malvern (3 Offices)		

Manchester	Oxford	Salcombe
(3 Offices)	Oxted	Sale
Margate	Paignton	Saltaire
Market Harborough	Parkstone	Saltash
Marlow	Peel (I. of Man)	Sandgate
Merthyr Tydfil	Penarth	Seaton
Middlesbrough	Penmaenmawr	Sevenoaks
Milford Haven	Pentre	Shifnal
Minehead	Penzance	Shipston-on-Stour
Modbury	Pershore	Shirley (Birmingham)
Monmouth	Plymouth	Sholey Bridge
Morley (Yorkshire)	Pontipool	Shrewsbury
Morpeth	Pontypool	Sidmouth
Mountain Ash	Pontypridd	Smethwick
Much Wenlock	Poole	Solihull
Neath	Port Dinorwic	Southam
Netherfield	Portsmouth	Southampton(3 Offices)
Netherton (Dudley)	Port. Talbot	Southborough
Newburn	Prestaigne	South Molton
Newcastle Emlyn	Purley	Southsea
Newcastle (Staffs.)	Ramsey (I. of Man)	South Shields
Newcastle-on-Tyne	Ramsgate	Spennymoor
(11 Offices)	Reading	Stafford
Newham	Redditch	Stanley (Co. Durham)
Newport (Mon.)	Redland (Bristol)	Staple Hill (Bristol)
do.—Maindee	Redruth	Stockton-on-Tees
Newport (Salop)	Rhymney	Stonehouse (Devon)
Newquay(Cornwall)	Romford	Stony Stratford
New Swindon	Ross	Stratford-on-Avon
Northampton	Rothbury	Stroud
North Shields	Ruagley	Sunderland (3 Offices)
Nottingham	Rye	Sutton Coldfield
Nuneaton	Ryton-on-Tyne	Swadlincote
Okehampton	St. Austell	Swanage
Oldbury	St. George's(Bristol)	Swansea
Old Hill	St. Ives (Cornwall)	Swindon
Oswestry	St. Leonards-on-Sea	Tamworth
Ottery St. Mary	St. Marychurch and	Taunton
	Babbacombe	Tavistock
		Teignmouth

Tenbury
Tenby
Tenterden
Tetbury
Tewkesbury
Thame
Tiverton
Tonbridge
Tonypandy
Torpoint
Torquay
Torre
Torrington
Totnes
Truro
Tunbridge Wells
Uttoxeter
Wallingford
Wallsend
Walsall
Warwick
Watford
Wealdstone
Wednesbury
Wellington (Salop)
Welshpool
West Bromwich
Westgate-on-Sea
Weymouth
Whitchurch (Salop)
Whitley Bay
Willenhall
Winslow
Wolverhampton
Worcester
Worthing
Wotton-under-Edge
Wrexham
And elsewhere

CURRENT ACCOUNTS are opened upon the terms usually adopted by Bankers.
DEPOSITS are received at interest, subject to notice of withdrawal, or by special
agreement. PURCHASES and SALES OF STOCKS effected through members
of the Stock Exchange, SECURITIES received for safe custody, COUPONS,
DIVIDENDS, PAY WARRANTS &c. collected, FOREIGN MONEYS exchanged,
periodical payments made, and every description of Banking business conducted.

THE BANK has CORRESPONDENTS and AGENTS throughout the British
Islands, to whom Credits can be paid by its Customers and others for transmission.
It has also a large number of COLONIAL and FOREIGN AGENTS, and undertakes the collection of FOREIGN BILLS and CHEQUES, and purchases approved
BILLS. LETTERS OF CREDIT and CIRCULAR NOTES are issued, and
FOREIGN CURRENCY DRAFTS, TELEGRAPHIC TRANSFERS, and LETTER
PAYMENTS, available in all parts of the world, can be obtained from the principal
Branches. The agency of COLONIAL and FOREIGN BANKS is undertaken.

THE BANK is prepared, in approved cases, to act as EXECUTOR and TRUSTEE
OF WILLS, TRUSTEE OF SETTLEMENTS, TRUSTEE OF DEBENTURE
STOCK ISSUES, &c. Copies of the regulations can be obtained from any of the
Offices.

A DECLARATION OF SECRECY is signed, on appointment, by every person
engaged in the Bank's service.

Branches of Lloyds Bank in January 1912 as listed in a deposit account passbook. The bank was then much smaller with head offices in London and Birmingham.

65

Huddersfield branch, 1914, of West Yorkshire Bank, prior to amalgamation with Lloyds Bank in September 1919.

Original premises of Beverley branch pictured in 1905 when known as 'Tiplady's Umbrella Infirmary'. Mr Tiplady, with the long clay pipe and whiskers, is standing in the doorway. Beverley branch was opened in 1957. Today the basement windows have gone and so have those steps but the front window of the branch maintains a similarity to its predecessor.

Exterior of Oxford branch, about 1930. The offices above are occupied by H. Donkin, Stock, Share & Insurance Broker. The glass window of the bank advertises World Wide Letters of Credit. Letters of credit were like travellers' cheques in that they enabled money to be drawn by the customer up to a fixed amount at particular foreign correspondents.

Market Place Reading branch, about 1945. In those days a branch was simply a place to withdraw and deposit money and negotiate an overdraft. Today a branch is a retail sales outlet selling a wide range of financial products from house insurance to pensions.

Hornby Road, Bombay branch, 1950. Pall Mall branch issued a booklet entitled Hints and Advice to Travellers and those proceeding to take up appointments in India and Burma. *On the question of servants it stated: 'Avoid, if possible, engaging a servant until arrival at your destination, and then be careful of the recommendations which applicants present, also make sure they refer to the actual man who applies to you. A personal recommendation from a brother officer of your service or firm is more satisfactory. A good servant as bearer to commence with in India makes your life easier, your clothes last longer and generally saves you money in many other ways, and, further, if you have to add to your staff at a later date he is likely to assist in the acquisition of a good and faithful menage.'*

Interior of Connaught Circus, New Delhi branch on a normal banking day, about 1953. Indian bearers can be seen waiting for their masters' cheques to be cashed. The bearer would bring in the cheque to be cashed and be given a brass token by the cashier. The signature on the cheque would then be checked and the balance of the account agreed before any money changed hands. This process often took a couple of hours to complete. The brass token was then handed over in exchange for the money.

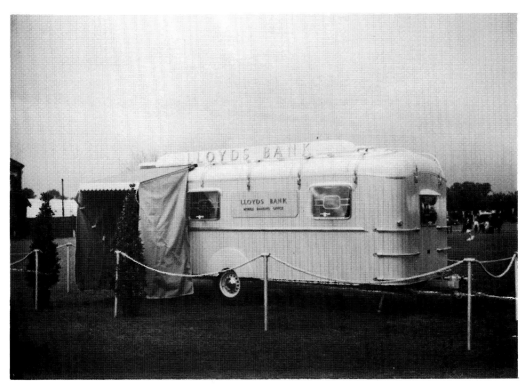

Mobile banking office, about 1955.

Cashier, Miss J. J. Tedstone, pictured at the first drive-in branch of Lloyds Bank at High Wycombe on Friday, 11 August 1961.

Staff of Commercial Road, Portsmouth, in the 1950s.

City Computer Centre, 1969.

Foreign exchange dealers, Cox & Co, 1919. Nowadays foreign exchange is a 24-hour market and the leisurely days of dealing in 1919 are gone forever. Today a dealer will start work at 6.30 am and work through to 6 pm.

Foreign exchange dealing room, Overseas Department, Eastcheap, 1969. Dealer, Charlie Frost, is seated nearest left. The flags displayed show which currency each dealer specialises in. The communication system seen above has long gone and been replaced by a single keyboard at each desk which can operate up to six multi-function screens. In todays dealing room millions of pounds worth of all the major currencies are bought and sold daily. Levels of activity can vary a lot from day to day. Some days are quiet when dealers end up staring at the screens like a zombie. Other days are very stressful with the action coming in waves, with bouts of hectic activity lasting for two hours or more.

Hay's Galleria, part of the new development called London Bridge City, which will eventually stretch the length of the south bank of the Thames from London Bridge to Tower Bridge. Hay's Lane House has been converted from a Victorian warehouse where tea clippers used to unload their cargoes, into modern offices for International Banking Division and the Marketing Department of UKRB. Picture taken 1986.

Black Horse Agencies Manager of the local Renton & Renton office in Leyburn, Ian Bebbington, measures up Hardraw Force in Yorkshire with Ian Harmer, a member of the Renton & Renton board of management. Negotiations for a sale at nearly £500,000 were put in hand in 1987 for the fall and nearby pub, The Green Dragon. The pub does well out of the fall as the only way to reach the beauty spot is through the bar! Black Horse Agencies originated in May 1982 when it acquired six offices. During 1987 its network size increased from 302 offices to 466 – an increase of 54 per cent.

Machines and Computers

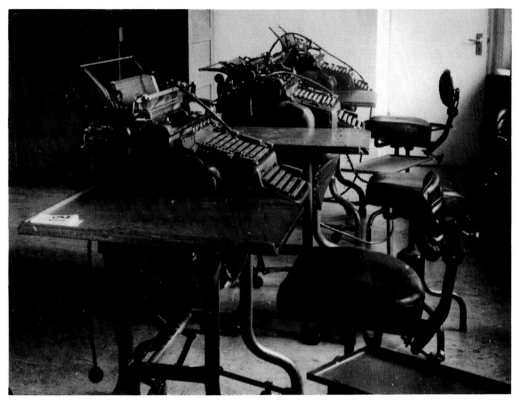

Three early 'posting machines' used at Five Ways, Birmingham. It was estimated that six male clerks could be replaced by five girls working machines at much lower salaries.

Powers Samas Punched Card Installation, Pall Mall, Mechanisation Department, about 1955. This system was installed on the fourth floor of the building and used for all ledger postings. These card tabulating machines were originally introduced as an experiment in 1938 to enable Pall Mall branch to cope with the expected increase in business handled on behalf of its Army customers that would accompany an outbreak of war. The machines could post a minimum of 800 entries an hour against only 75 if done by hand.

The Bank's First Computer

The Dark Horse magazine reported in 1962 that current account posting by computer had arrived. At Pall Mall branch, over 16,000 current accounts were maintained on a computer and later in that year a second computer went into action. By May 1963, all the current accounts, some 57,000, were fed into the new machines. Up to 15,000 entries a day were made at a posting speed of 2,500 per hour.

The computer chosen by the Bank for this first installation was an IBM RAMAC (Random Access Method of Accounting and Control). Discs retained a record in magnetic form. The input was by conventional punched card. No daily ledger and statement sheets were printed out as these were produced only as required on a diary basis, all the information being retained in the computer itself. This information, however, could be made available in a matter of seconds through a special enquiry system which had been installed; hence the words 'Random Access'. This particular system was far in advance of any known method in use in Britain at that time. Pall Mall was fully computerised by the summer of 1963.

The magazine concluded their report as follows:

'For readers who expect some facetious comment on the name of this inhuman machine, and who think that accounting and control is already frequently a haphazard operation, it is well to notice that the *Oxford English Dictionary* says that "random" means "great speed" before it means "without purpose".'

The computer printer of Lloyds Bank's IBM RAMAC installation. This machine printed customers' statements and ledger sheets.

Engineer adjusting access arm in magnetic disc file of IBM RAMAC Computer.

The Punch Room. Here information was transferred onto punched cards to be fed into the computer.

The Miscellaneous Machine Section of the Random Access Machine Accounting System.

A remote enquiry station of the IBM Random Access Machine Accounting System. The computer installation was on the third floor but at stations like this in other parts of the building the balance of any account could be ascertained within seconds.

The computer console. The operator is seen controlling the work of the computer.

A remote enquiry station of the IBM Random Access Machine Accounting System at Cox's & King's Branch. Pictured are: G. B. Hague, Inspector (Research); G. C. Watkins, Manager, Cox's & King's Branch; Harald Peake, (Deputy) Chairman Lloyds Bank; Field Marshall Sir Gerald Templar, Director of the Bank and a member of the Pall Mall Committee; Air Chief Marshal Sir James Robb, member of the Pall Mall Committee.

Prototype of the new automatic cashier, known as Cashpoint, which the Bank introduced to its branches in 1972. The initial order was for 500 machines at a total cost of £3½ million. Cashpoint was the first automatic cash dispenser in the world to be linked to a computerised branch banking network. The first machines dispensed variable amounts of cash up to a £20 limit which was later raised to £100 a day, provided the customer had sufficient funds. The cost of each automatic cashier varied between £5,800 and £7,750 depending on the type of installation in the branch. The first machine was operative in Brentwood, 11 December 1972.

Staff Memories

L. G. A. Buchanan (retired) wrote to *Lloyds Bank News* in 1985:

'While I was a cashier at Cheltenham branch in the 1930s, I used to chat to a pensioner who had been manager at the Capital & Counties Bank, Stroud.

Soon after the take-over in, I think, 1918 the Lloyds Bank Inspectors arrived one afternoon after 15.00. When told the Manager was hunting, the Inspectors became rather annoyed.

Next morning, the Manager was informed that his fox hunting would cease forthwith. The Manager – I believe his name was Baxter, had other ideas. He wrote to the Chairman of Lloyds Bank, Sir Richard Vassar-Smith and explained his feelings.

Sir Richard replied that he should continue to hunt, as he was sure that the Manager's presence in the hunting field was good for the Bank.'

Working for Lloyds Bank proved to be an unhappy experience for some as Alfred H. Phipps recalled in 1980 in a letter to the Chairman:

'In 1916 I joined the staff of Lloyds Bank Ltd, at a princely salary of £40 per annum. Some two years later I received my calling-up papers, and was duly conscripted into the Army. By that time I had attained the rank of Chief Junior, and was also the proud possessor of a personal letter from the then Chairman commending me for having continued to deliver out from a waiting taxi the weeks cash approximating £80,000 in notes, silver, and copper which had been collected by the Branch Messenger and myself from Head Office, after the first bomb ever to be dropped on London in daylight had just exploded at the corner of Fenchurch Avenue. I am happy to say that no human lives were lost, but a delivery van horse lying dead in the road about 30 yards from our taxi bore witness to the effectiveness of the bomb. I should add that the Bank Messenger who was taking the money into the bank by trolley also received a similar letter from the Chairman.

On the eve of my departure from the bank, my colleagues presented me with a fountain pen as a token of their esteem and goods wishes, and I also received a cheque of £10 from Mr Martin, the Bank Manager, that being the agreed practice on the part of Lloyds Bank Ltd, in respect of all members of the staff joining HM Forces. It is needless to say how pleased I was to receive those gifts that came as a complete surprise.

A few weeks later while in camp at Brockton, Staffordshire, I received an apologetic letter from Mr Waters, Assistant Manager to Mr Martin, explaining that the gift of £10 only applied to permanent members of the staff, and, as my appointment had been on a temporary basis, the gift should not have been made in my case. Would I, therefore, please return the amount in question. As you may well imagine, such an unchristian-like act both shocked and disgusted me, especially as Mr Waters' letter was the first intimation that my appointment had been a temporary one, and, as the months passed, my feeling towards the Bank grew less and less warm, so much so that, when I was eventually demobilised in April, 1920, I had long since decided that my future would be better and more safely employed with a less uncharitable organisation. I should add, that, when I called on Mr Martin to explain why I was not returning, he made every effort to make me change my mind, even resorting to the suggestion that, in leaving, I was committing an act of commercial suicide. However, I remained adamant, and duly bid my farewell to Manager and Staff.'

However, the recollections of the late Leslie E. Bickel, OBE in his book *Flying, Banking and Music – Recollections of a Varied Life* were a lot happier:

'I left school at the end of 1914 and wanted to train as a teacher. My parents, however, still found life difficult financially and with both older brothers in the Services, there were insufficient funds to support me through college. So banking was my choice of career, and I duly presented myself at Salisbury as one of the last juniors to be interviewed by the two Chief General Managers of the former Wilts and Dorset Bank, H. S. Harbridge and Walter Moon. Although by that time the bank had been absorbed by Lloyds, it was still functioning independently.

I started at the Winton branch when postal orders were legal tender and gold still circulated freely. It's a telling comment on present conditions when security guards in hard helmets deliver money in armoured cars, to realise that the other junior and I used to take the surplus cash to Bournemouth in open horse and trap with the copper and silver bags at our feet and the gold clutched to our chests.

Our manager, Reginald Case, was a farmer's son from Winfrith in Dorset and banking hours sat lightly upon him; he went shooting regularly twice a week. Shooting was in fact so much part of his life that one day when I pointed out that the fire in his private room was smoking badly, without any ado he pulled a revolver from his hip pocket and put a bullet up the chimney, saying "That'll bring the soot down"!

Working conditions were far more leisurely then; all book-keeping entries were hand-posted and the copying of letters had to be hand-pressed. At balance times, twice a year, we worked till two and three in the morning with never a suggestion of overtime pay. It would be the manager's wife who would bring us the cups of tea to aid us in our work.

Demobilisation on 5 February 1919 took me back to Bournemouth as a junior clerk at Lloyds Bank, Winton, to fill inkpots and change blotting paper at a salary of £60 per year. Even so, with the service gratuity I received and the money I had saved while in France, I was able to buy a Douglas motor cycle. We had no civilian clothes, so for weeks had to wear our army uniforms in the Bank while suits were being made. Ready-mades were of the future and not till the end of the Second World War were demobilisation suits provided.

Very changed were the conditions from those I had left. Many of the staff were female, and from those at that branch who had joined up, only I had returned unscathed. W. Omer Cooper, a ledger clerk, had been killed in the Somme battles; Jimmy Andrews, cashier, had lost a leg; John Rich, cashier, had been taken prisoner and died later from his experiences; and Arthur Brooks, joint junior with me, had been blinded. He later returned to Bournemouth main branch as a Braille typist. All had joined the Bankers' Battalion of the Royal Fusiliers.

Tich Wooldridge, another ledger clerk, had also joined the Bankers' Battalion, but as his height and breadth were roughly identical, he caused a bottleneck in the trenches and was transferred to a clerical post at the base where, he told me later, he had enjoyed the time of his life. He served in the same company as Tom Webster, the famous *Daily Mail* cartoonist who published a magazine in France, known as the *Bankers' Draft*. In this was included a caricature of Tich.

Tich lived in Southbourne, yet walked to and from Winton to work, always wearing breeches and gaiters. His main source of sustenance was strong ale, and in the evenings he would walk from Bournemouth to Christchurch or Poole calling at various hostelries en route. He had been brought up on a Wiltshire farm and as a young man had been an amateur jockey and prize-fighter. When serving at a South Wales branch he had had the misfortune to lay out his manager following a divergence of opinion over book-keeping procedure. As his family were important customers of the Wilts & Dorset Bank he did not lose his job but was transferred to Bridport branch where the manager himself was no mean exponent of the noble art, and after business hours Tich told me they would enjoy sparring practice in the manager's room.

In October 1919, Lloyds Bank, Bournemouth, was the first bank in the area to establish a Sports Club and I was elected captain of football. The club is still flourishing.

We played on Read's Muscliffe farm, changing our gear at the *Horse and Jockey* hotel opposite; clubs in the Bournemouth and District Football League were our opponents. I enjoyed playing both football and cricket for many years, but my only claim to fame was as wicket-keeper for Lloyds Country Team against their London side in 1926 at New Beckenham.

Freddie Weaver, who was at Charminster Road in the 20s and early 1930s was a protégé of Dr W. G. Grace and played cricket many times for Gloucestershire, once taking nine wickets in an innings against Yorkshire. He was one of the fastest bowlers and hardest hitters playing in the Bournemouth district. He took out a special insurance policy covering himself against the very many claims he received for smashed windows in Maxwell Road when playing at Winton recreation ground.

My father died in the early 1920s and within a year or so my mother moved house to Moordown. With my brother Harold in India and Claude killed, I became mainly responsible for the household which included my sister Doreen and younger brother Maurice. I therefore welcomed the formation of the local branch of the Institute of Bankers as a means of assistance in study for its examinations. That meant correspondence courses and working at night in my bedroom with an oil lamp to provide both heat and light. In 1924, having completed both parts of my Institute examinations, I was appointed to open a new sub-branch at Moordown.

It was in the 1920s that two murders occured at sub-branches of Lloyds Bank, one at Ferryhill in the north of England and the other at Bordon Camp in Hampshire. Sub-branch clerks were later protected by guards and warning alarm bells. These bells however were not always used in the manner intended – as one Inspector is reported later to have discovered. Visiting a sub-branch, he asked whether the alarm was working properly and was assured that it had been tested that very morning and found satisfactory. The Inspector insisted upon testing the bell himself, but was somewhat startled to obtain a rather unexpected response: a waiter arrived from the pub opposite bearing a tray with a couple of pints of foaming ale!

By 1929 business at the sub-branch had grown to such an extent that I was appointed Clerk-In-Charge under the Winton manager. Subsequently it was raised to the status of a full branch and a more senior man was appointed, I having insufficient experience for full management. His tenure however was short; his health broke down and I was given sole control. It was then that I handled gold in any quantity. One incident I recall was of a horse-dealer who brought in 100 golden sovereigns which he had received from some gypsies in the New Forest to whom he had sold a pony. I pointed out to him that by taking the coins to a bullion dealer in the town he could double their value, but "No", he insisted, "That would not be honest", demanding that I bank them at their face value.

It was interesting to watch the development of heathland into a prosperous suburb, and satisfying to have been instrumental in the development of various businesses, some of which are now firmly established.

In the early 1920s, the Royal Aero Club organised an Air Race meeting at Ensbury Park. One of the turning points in the race circuit was at Wood Town Farm, West Parley, owned by Mr Trelawney Dayrell-Reed, then president of the Dorset Poetry Society and a close friend of Augustus John, the celebrated artist who at the time lived at Alderley Manor. The two of them regularly used to play shove-ha'penny together at *The Horns Inn* at West Parley.

Mr Reed was so enraged by the deafening noise of the aeroplanes circling his farm that he got out his shotgun and peppered the wings of a competitor's Sopwith Camel. He was subsequently charged at Dorchester Assizes with attempted manslaughter. However, a host of artistic friends who recalled the old saying "And shall Trelawney die? Twenty thousand Cornishmen shall know the reason why" came to his assistance and he was finally cleared upon grounds of extreme provocation.

After the aerodrome was closed a company was formed to construct a racecourse but that lasted for only about a year. During that period I handled more counterfeit coins and forged treasury notes than in all the remaining years of my banking life.

In 1935 came promotion to management of Malmesbury Park branch in Holdenhurst Road. Here many of the accounts were held by substantial local ground landlords, and I had considerable experience in dealing with leasehold properties. But this was a time of slump. Lending against leaseholds with falling prices was risky and I was faced with entirely new conditions, totally different from those at Moordown. Holdenhurst Road, once a main artery into Bournemouth, suffered a steady decline awaiting the decision (delayed for years) for the construction of what is now Wessex Way. Had Castle Lane been developed from Iford through Kinson and Bear Cross it would surely have provided a better ring road for Bournemouth? For the final outcome cut Malmesbury Park in half and caused tremendous disruption.

September 1939 saw the outbreak of the Second World War, but this time banks were better prepared than in 1914. Each branch was allotted a custodian branch to which complete duplicate records were sent every night so that should one branch suffer from enemy action, its transactions could be obtained from another. How beneficial a scheme this proved to be was demonstrated when customers escaping to the mainland from the Channel Islands before the invasion were able to obtain up-to-date statements and operate their accounts immediately.

1945 saw the end of the war, and this time returning bank staff appeared in demobilisation suits. Thankfully, but sadly, only one of my staff, Wills, a junior clerk, had been killed. He had been a battle pilot flying Hurricanes and on 4 September 1940, had written to me giving a graphic account of his first engagement with the enemy; he was killed the very next day.

More gentle was life at the Bank in those days. One customer from my Home Guard platoon who ran a dairy would pop his head round the door of my room, come to attention, and say "Good Morning Sarge". Lord Malmesbury, a regular visitor at the branch, always on entering would take off his hat and coat before going to the counter. Laying down his umbrella he would then bow to the cashier. The courtesies would be exchanged by the cashier locking his till and going round the counter to hold the door open for the departing visitor. Alas! such courtesies are not possible today with staff having to be confined behind protective screens.

Never through all the years in Bournemouth was I tempted to apply for a move which might have taken me to another part of the country. What more could I desire for than the opportunity of attending symphony concerts, of taking part in music making, and of enjoying the sea and Hampshire cricket? Imagine my pleasure when I was offered the managership of Winton, the branch at which I had started in 1915. So it was in 1950, 35 years after my first entry into the Winton branch, that I took control of it. One member of the staff, Cyril Pitman, who returned to the branch after being a prisoner in the First World War, was still there as Accountant. Strange was the sensation of sitting in the managerial chair!

On one occasion, when chairman of the local branch of the Save the Children Fund, I invited Freddie Mills to open an event of ours. He was a Bournemouth man and this was soon after he had won the World Light-Heavyweight title. Rising to his feet after I had introduced him, he turned and surveyed his surroundings, and then said; "The last time I was at this house I was delivering the milk". Thus was the fête declared open!

I enjoyed my days in banking. To meet people in all walks of life, to be able to help many over difficulties, and gain an insight into local affairs was tremendously satisfying. Bankers are like doctors and ministers of religion. Customers know that they can turn to them in any emergency, completely confident in the pledge of secrecy. I learned that one of the greatest gifts a bank manager can possess is to be able to say "No" nicely, to refuse a request without giving offence.

I served upon the local committee of the Institute of Bankers for over thirty years and was president of the local centre throughout the years of the last war, but since I retired in 1958 banking has developed widely and is now international in character. Computers have taken over control of routine work, and competition between the large banks is very keen. How different from my Wilts & Dorset days!'

R. F. S. Kipling, now retired, recalls his junior days in 1941 when he joined the Bank:

'Inspite of low pay and staff shortages, because of the war, it was an exciting time. As a very junior clerk, I had to attend the "Local Clearing"' where cheques drawn on local banks were exchanged and settlements made. A clerk from each bank attended with listings of cheques on every bank – these would be exchanged, listing and cheques checked, and balances struck. Any clerk who could not "balance" his settlements within a tight time limit had to pay a fine of one penny for every minute that he was still wrong! This was quite unofficial, and when there was sufficient in the "kitty" cream buns were bought for the next "clearing".

Those early days recall the un-worried way we used to carry cash around – no bullion vans then. As junior I had to go as clerk and escort to a sub-branch which opened twice a week (Honley, I think sub to Huddersfield) and on a Friday we went by taxi stopping to deliver the wages to a large mill on our way. Whilst the taxi-driver acted as escort to the cashier, I was left in the taxi (in the mill yard) guarding the sub-branch cash alone!'

Len Bickley from Thame branch recalls the day an attractive young lady called at one of his previous branches. Eager to assist he said 'Good afternoon. Can I help at all?' The attractive customer replied 'My doctors away, can I see you instead?' 'Yes by all means my dear' replied Len. 'Just come into this interview room and take off all your clothes.' 'I beg you pardon!' the customer retorted. 'Now you stop and think about it', said Len. 'You told me that your doctor is away and asked could I see you instead. Now whether or not I do you any good I don't know, but if you wish me to examine you take off all your clothes.' 'Oh no', she replied, 'I only want my passport signed!'

When Len was working at the Kingsbridge branch he recollects a particularly bad time, about 1953, when the branch was almost unable to open because of staff sickness. The nearby Midland Bank was unaffected. Someone from his office had the bright idea of ringing up Midland and asking for a cashier. Len states: 'So we had a Midland Bank cashier running our counter for a day. He did a good job too! It raised a few eyebrows amongst the customers but at least they had someone there to look after them. God knows what the inspectors would have said!'

Patrick Richards concludes with his banking memories written shortly before he retired in 1987:

'I joined Lloyds Bank in 1961 as a late entrant and my first branch was a branch in London. For a fortnight I was the office junior whose task consisted of keeping the savings bank and deposit account ledgers up straight, making all the necessary entries, doing the post at night, keeping the ink wells filled in the banking hall. We were still using nibbed pens and ordinary ink in those days and making sure the blotting-paper was clean.

The branch was run by a man whose title was then the Accountant. In other branches he was known as the Chief Clerk. The only difference between the two titles appeared to be the Accountant was under 35 and was usually an up and coming man in the banking world, and the Chief Clerk was over 50 and had probably reached the highest point in his banking career that he was going to reach.

The Manager was a remote figure who only appeared from his office once during the day to sign the Head Office Letter. This ritual ran as follows: As soon as the Waste Clerk had balanced the waste and had written the Head Office Letter the Accountant was informed. He then checked it through and signed it and then went to inform the Manager. Before the latter appeared from his office the Accountant called for silence in the general office for the Manager to sign the Head Office Letter. At this the rest of the staff were expected to cease whatever task they were in engaged in, stand up while the Manager proceeded through the banking hall, round the back of the counter to the waste desk. Silence was maintained while he added up and checked the letter, added his signature and returned to his office. Once the door had closed the Accountant then said, "Carry on everyone".

In spite of this daily procedure it was a fortnight before the Manager even noticed me. One afternoon on returning from signing the Head Office Letter he suddenly realised there was a strange face amongst those in the office, and stopping short in front of me he said, "Who are you?" Before I could reply the Accountant hastily stepped forward and effected introductions. This interruption to his routine over, the Manager returned to his office, and it was about three months before he spoke to me again.

He was, I now realise, what must have been one of the last of the dying breed of pre-war bank managers. He invariably wore striped trousers and a black jacket and only ever saw the richest customers. Customers called at the bank to see him and no occasion did I ever know of him to go out and visit them.

As Christmas approached there was a steady stream of customers all bearing gifts, beating a path to his door. In fact for the two weeks before Christmas he brought in a large suitcase which was taken home each night full of whatever goodies had been presented to him during the day. The only time that the staff shared in any of the presents that were given to him, was when the local greengrocer presented him with a crate of oranges and the staff, which consisted of about 25 people, was each given one orange.

After doing the junior job in the office for a while I was eventually allowed onto the counter as a cashier. My training for this consisted of being handed a till with some money in and being told to count it. I was given a till sheet and told credits go on the left, payments out go in the middle column for customers of other branches and in the right-hand column if they are our customers. I was then left for the rest of the day to serve customers. When the bank closed I was told to count my money and add up the columns on my sheet and providing everything balanced I was then a fully qualified cashier. With such training as this it will come as no surprise that after about a week I had a ten pound short. At this time, every difference in cash had to be reported to Head Office on a Form 7, which had to be signed by the manager in person. His only comment on my presenting the form to him for signature was, "It's a pity this had to happen at this stage in your career". I felt I was doomed!

This particular manager had also carried on a feud with the number two securities clerk for some years. No-one appeared to know what had started this feud, but neither had spoken to the other except through a third party during the whole of this time. When the time came for the Manager to retire he arranged a small reception for the staff and various selected customers in a room in the hotel opposite the branch. He went round to each member of staff in turn inviting them to attend this function. The Second Securities Clerk was left till last, and we all waited with bated breath to see whether the silence of years would be broken. Eventually the Manager took the plunge and approaching the Securities Clerk said, "As you know I am holding a small party for my retirement and I wonder if you would care to attend". There was the briefest of pauses and then the reply, "No!". The Manager retired in haste to his office.

I have already said this Manager always wore striped trousers and jacket. The dress for ordinary members of the staff, male members that is, consisted of a dark suit, a plain white shirt with a detachable stiff collar, and a plain or striped tie of sober hue. One day the young man who succeeded me as office junior appeared in the office wearing a grey suit with a small checked pattern. Unfortunately the Manager caught sight of this and the junior was sent home to change immediately with the admonition that only bookmakers and people of that sort wore checked suits.

Twice a year on balance nights we were expected, or rather required, to stay until the work was finished. This was usually somewhere around midnight. For this no overtime was paid but the Manager bought us sandwiches, with beer for the men, sherry for the ladies. For the rest of the year one stayed until the work was finished, which meant that the last ledger had been checked to the last statement and all the post had gone. Now as the post office closed at 6.30 pm the final letter to be sent came out of the Manager's office at around 6.28 pm. Whoever was on post then had the task of trying to cross the Marylebone Road during the evening rush hour, and then running the remaining 50 yards down Baker Street to the post office before the doors were closed.

The next manager we had was a totally different proposition. He had spent the last 10 years or so in a quiet little number in Head Office and was due for retirement but had been talked into staying on for two years to manage the branch during the advent of the computer. All he wanted was a quiet life and so his first act was to acquire an assistant manager to do the work while he sat around and read the newspaper, and went for the occasional stroll in the nearby Regents Park.

Well we're now into what was termed the swinging sixties and the formality of dress was now relaxing slightly, especially on Saturday mornings when grey flannels and blazers or sports jackets could be worn. Our new manager on the rare Saturdays on which he came in took to sporting a spotted bow-tie. However, he stopped this when on one Saturday the rest of the staff turned up all wearing bow-ties.

This manager was a gentleman, and what might be termed one of the old school and not really with it in the terms of the swinging sixties, and consequently we decided that his outlook should be broadened. When one of our best customers, who were a group of theatrical agents handling pop stars, brought in a certain well known lead singer who I shall call Mr X, we decided that our manager was the very person to see him to open an account into which this celebrity was going to place all his new found wealth which was considerable. Mr X had with him an extremely attractive young blonde lady who he called darling, but did not bother to introduce. We went to the manager's office and said, "We've got Mr X outside and he wants to open an account. We're sure you'd like to see him". He said "Who is Mr X?" and we said, "Well he's the lead singer of the pop group "The – – –". It was perfectly obvious that he'd never heard either of the group or of Mr X, but he was game for anything. So coming out into the banking hall where the celebrity was now signing autographs for admiring female members of the staff, he stepped forward with his hand extended, shook Mr X warmly by the hand and said "Ah, how do you do Mr X?" and turning to the blonde young lady said, "And this I presume is Mrs X?" His face was a picture when Mr X said "Na, this is the bird what I lives with".

It was shortly after this event that I received my transfer to a branch in Hertfordshire, though I don't think the two events were connected, as the Manager invited me back to his retirement party shortly after that. The manager in my new branch at that time was a pillar of the local community and a leading light in the local Rotary Club. Now the Rotary Club organised the annual carnival which took place on a Saturday afternoon and in which most of the town was involved in one way or another.

The carnival procession went from the town centre and travelled round various outlying districts, a distance of several miles before returning to the town centre, collecting money during the whole of their trip. The staff at the bank were told by the Manager that they could be expected to attend the branch during the Saturday afternoon of the carnival to receive and count and bag up the money which had been collected. As this was a charity event the staff would not receive any remuneration and anyone being bold enough to defy him and not appear would get some remark like "unco-operative" on their annual report and most certainly not get a rise. During the three years until his retirement no member of the staff of Lloyds Bank was able to see or take part in the carnival as they were shut in the branch counting money until after six o'clock in the evening.

This manager was also firmly convinced that he was the only one who knew anything about banking or could handle any particular job in the office. He therefore constantly interferred with every department and generally drove everyone mad.

His successor was quite normal, and consequently didn't stay long but moved on after about three years to bigger and better things and in turn we acquired another eccentric.

This particular manager was again one who was only interested in seeing the richest customers, but not for the reasons you might think. His one aim in life was to be taken out to lunch everyday with the lunch being paid for by the customer and it was quite amazing how whenever he had managed to inveigle a customer into taking him to lunch, his wife and on several occasions his son would also just happen to appear in the office at lunchtime, and what could the poor unfortunate customer do, but include them in his invitation.

We had over the years developed the custom that when anybody left the branch, for whatever reason, we would hold a sherry party after work in the rest-room to bid the member of staff farewell. Food as well as drinks were served at this party, and it was amazing how on every occasion that one of these events was held the manager's wife and son also just happened to drop in around five o'clock, so that they could also partake of the food and drink. There are no records of the Manager ever inviting a member of staff or a customer to his house for a meal.

As I now approach my retirement I think back on that first manager that I knew in London and remember one last story. About six weeks before his actual retirement he wrote letters to every one of over 3,000 customers pointing out that his retirement was due, and that should they wish to contribute to his retirement present, cheques and cash would be received by the first securities clerk, either by post or during banking hours. The sheer unmitigated cheek of this left most of us speechless. However, it had the desired effect and the Manager finally retired with his bank balance swollen by a rather considerable sum.'

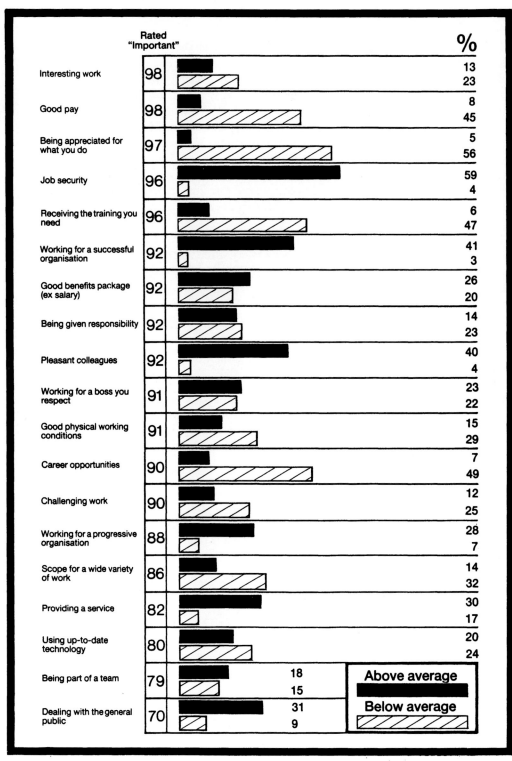

Rated "Important"		%
Interesting work	98	13 / 23
Good pay	98	8 / 45
Being appreciated for what you do	97	5 / 56
Job security	96	59 / 4
Receiving the training you need	96	6 / 47
Working for a successful organisation	92	41 / 3
Good benefits package (ex salary)	92	26 / 20
Being given responsibility	92	14 / 23
Pleasant colleagues	92	40 / 4
Working for a boss you respect	91	23 / 22
Good physical working conditions	91	15 / 29
Career opportunities	90	7 / 49
Challenging work	90	12 / 25
Working for a progressive organisation	88	28 / 7
Scope for a wide variety of work	86	14 / 32
Providing a service	82	30 / 17
Using up-to-date technology	80	20 / 24
Being part of a team	79	18 / 15
Dealing with the general public	70	31 / 9

Above average (black bar)
Below average (hatched bar)

In February 1987, 12,354 members of staff were sent a MORI questionnaire – all managers and a randomly selected sample of all other categories of staff working in this country. About 8,500 forms were returned. The above chart shows some of the results of this survey. The first column of figures rates the importance (out of 100) the staff gave to each of the things that a job can offer. The black bars tell how many thought Lloyds Bank was above average in this respect while the hatched bars record the percentage who think the Bank falls below average.

Bank Staff

A typical bank around 1800 would have consisted of a country establishment near a market place having an outer office with a counter, and an internal parlour. The parlour was where the active partners worked. The clerks in the outer office would be lifelong servants of the firm with no prospects of promotion to the parlour. The clerks would have been nominated when they were boys by someone with family or business connections with the bank.

After the legislative changes of 1826 and 1833 joint stock banks began to appear. This expansion of the banking profession meant that trained bank staff were in greater demand. Each bank found itself losing men to its competitors. For example, the County of Gloucester Bank in 1839 raised its head clerk's salary as he had been offered a place in a new joint stock bank in London. The next year they poached a clerk from their rivals the Gloucestershire Banking Company.

Eventually the banks took matters into their own hands in the form of restrictive agreements. By 1900 the Capital & Counties Bank, which was later acquired by Lloyds Bank, enforced upon all the staff of absorbed banks a clause preventing employees from joining another bank within 15 miles, for a period of a year on leaving a Capital & Counties office.

The long-term solution of the staffing problem was to recruit juniors for training by offering an attractive career. From 1870 onwards it was recognised as the normal way of keeping staff. However, there were still movements from bank to bank especially in the appointment of managers and members of old banking families still managed to jump the queue.

By the 1850s there were still many banks where a family atmosphere predominated. For example, a partner at Twinings, which became the Law Courts branch of Lloyds Bank in the Strand, upon taking on an apprentice wrote to the boy's father: 'He would board and lodge in our house and an exact conformity to the rules and reputations of the family would be expected from him, as from others.' The clerk would have every opportunity to learn the business in the outer office but it would have been almost impossible to obtain promotion to manager.

Bank clerks were not very well paid. During their apprenticeship they were paid at £10, £20 or £30 a year in the country. After serving their apprenticeship a clerk might expect to earn £30 or £40 in the country with £60 or £70 in London. Eventually the clerk might expect to earn £100 or even £150. Upon promotion to cashier or accountant his salary would be £150 or £200. Salaries of between £200 and £400 were paid in the West End business of Harries Farquhar and Company.

Salaries were often supplemented by family and friends. An employee with independent means had an advantage. In 1861 the Gloucestershire Banking Company appointed a clerk at £150 a year 'upon the understanding that on his marriage he will have at least £100 a year of his wife's'.

Dependence on part-time workers was important in the middle of the 19th century. The new joint stock banks would establish themselves in a town by opening an agency, which could later be converted to a branch. Often the man appointed to act as agent was a man with substantial business contacts in the town. He would be allowed to continue his previous occupation until such time as the agency was turned into a branch, when he would then become full-time manager. However, there were disadvantages to this system. In 1840 a branch manager was requested by the Directors of the Gloucestershire Banking Company to devote more time to the business of the bank and less to his practice as a surveyor. In return the bank offered to increase his salary. The North Wilts Banking Company asked their General Manager to give up his legal practice. He refused to do this but agreed to devote more time to visiting the outlying branches.

By the turn of the century paid employment or trading outside the bank was forbidden except for agency work for insurance companies and farming. In 1891 Howard Lloyd had expressed some anxiety about branch managers holding 'Insurance Agency Appointments and working them unduly'. He regretted that little could be done about the situation as 'the practice had become of some standing'. This practice remained until very recently whereby a local manager, subject to sanction by Head Office, could hold an insurance agency.

Farming was customarily allowed. Rural branches tended to be to some extent a law unto themselves. In order for a manager to gain respect of the local farmers he had to know about farming. There are many examples, particularly in the West Country, where bank managers were also farmers. Sometimes the local manager was not the only farmer in the branch. For example, in the 1870s the manager of the Stow-on-the-Wold branch of the Gloucestershire Banking Company had a farm some six miles away from the branch. He spent much of his time running it while his cashier looked after his farm next door to the bank.

From early 1917 until November 1925, T. S. Eliot, the famous poet and literary critic, worked as a clerk in Lloyds Bank, spending much of his time in the then Colonial and Foreign Department where his knowledge of French and Italian was invaluable. He spent his early days filing balance sheets for £2.10s (£2.50) a week. His evenings were spent lecturing, writing poetry and reviewing books. Eliot's poem, *The Waste Land*, which drew on his time with the Bank, was published in 1922 and hailed as 'revolutionary' by the literary world of the time.

Eliot's pay in 1922 was £455 a year and there is a note on his staff file made by Mr Harrison, General Manager in charge of administration that 'The question of an increase in Mr Eliot's salary should not be dealt with unless Mr Eliot raised the question himself'.

One thing is clear from T. S. Eliot's letters – he greatly enjoyed his job in the Bank. However, he did leave the Bank in 1925 to join the publishing firm of Faber and Faber.

Inspectors

G. W. Baldwin, Chief Inspector 1901–1913. He started his banking career at High Street, Birmingham and for years afterwards customers remembered him as one of the best cashiers ever on the counter of that branch.

The first Inspection Clerk was appointed in 1872. One of the first branches inspected was Rugby and the General Manager of Lloyds Banking Company Limited wrote to the Manager of the branch as follows: 'You will kindly allow him free access to everything at your Branch, and give him any assistance necessary. He will be expressly enjoined to act with the greatest deference and respect to yourself and every Branch Manager.'

Over the years more inspectors were appointed. The 1903 Staff List mentions seven inspectors of branches based at the Birmingham Head Office in Edmund Street. These were George Tyler, W. J. Burden, A. Davidson, W. C. Buckley, A. V. Williams, A. G. Barker and John Counsell. The Chief Inspector was G. W. Baldwin who was the most famous of the early chief inspectors.

Mr Baldwin was born in 1849 and entered the Bank at High Street, Birmingham in 1869, becoming manager at Deritend 10 years later. He became an inspector in 1889 and was Chief Inspector from 1901 to 1913. The expansion of the Bank took place after he joined the inspection staff. Amalgamations of banks were no longer confined to the neighbourhood of Birmingham. The preliminary arrangements were made by the Directors, the Chairman and the General Manager leaving the inspectors with the difficult task of the details to see to. In the *Lloyds Bank Magazine* it was reported that: 'Mr Baldwin was generally in charge. Often away from home for long periods, he never let his own comfort or convenience come before his severe conception of this duty to the Bank. His work took him at short notice into a strange district, with unfamiliar customs and trades, where he had to assist in examining and reporting on accounts and securities of all kinds; to initiate at once into a new system of book-keeping the more than bewildered clerks, accustomed to a different method; to decide instantly on every conceivable question of routine and administration, and, most difficult of all, to do this in such a way as to hurt no susceptibility, but to bring everybody, customers, partners and clerks alike into willing acquiescence with the change.'

Only one inspector for the London District is mentioned in the 1903 Staff List and his name is W. W. Mitchell based at the London Head Office, 71 Lombard Street. By 1918 there were 22 staff and 32 in 1948. Today there are over 300 staff.

In the early days the Assistant Inspector had to type the branch reports and they had to be typed without a mistake. They had to set an example to the rest of the staff so making an error and rubbing it out was not good enough. One incorrect word meant that the whole report had to be retyped. Nowadays, inspectors no longer have to type their own reports.

The introduction and rapid growth of computer technology has seen the expansion of a computer audit team, which now has 40 inspectors and staff. Another team of 12 is reserved specially for inspecting branches abroad. Its members are supported by domestic inspection staff. Besides requiring a high level of broad banking skills and language abilities this team of inspectors require a high degree of interpersonal skills to enable them to cope with the logistics and procedures necessary for inspecting these foreign branches. Inspectors have to be able to identify the local customs and their implications very quickly.

It is interesting to note that Brazil has one system of book-keeping laid down by the Central Bank of Brazil and it has to be strictly adhered to. However, Head Office returns have to follow the Lloyds Bank system. The consequence is that both methods run side by side.

Today inspectors and their teams are generally respected for the role they perform and are regarded as professionals. They aim to leave the branch a much better place than they found it by bringing an independent and outside point of view. Over the past two decades they have departed from the audit/security role towards the guide and counsellor role. The emphasis today is on risk/cost effectiveness and being user-orientated as it is the branch that has to pay the cost of the inspection.

One Lloyds Bank branch has a clear memory of the day when the Inspector called. The main problem was that he was from Barclays Bank. Having settled down to work he came to the conclusion, after half-an-hour, that the documents before him referred rather consistently to Lloyds Bank. He quickly made his excuses and left.

Staff of Gloucester office, about 1880. In Victorian times clerks were prohibited from becoming security for any other person, were forbidden to gamble and expected to act at all times with 'zeal, activity and assiduity'.

Staff of the old Swindon and new Swindon branches of Capital and Counties Bank Limited, 1894. Back row: F. S. Wilson, C. Sneath, E. T. J. Badcock, H. C. Cook. Second row: H. T. Dixon, E. Ing, T. Byrch, C. R. Baily, H. Rivers. D. C. Waddy is pictured in front.

Telephone No. 1.

COVENTRY CITY POLICE.

WANTED,

In this City, on Warrant, charged with falsification of accounts, thereby obtaining a very large amount of money, belonging to his employers, Lloyds' Banking Company, Ltd.,

JOSEPH STEPHEN WEATHERILT

(A BANKER'S ACCOUNTANT CLERK).

Photo taken 20 years ago, but would now be a good   likeness if the man was clean shaven.

DESCRIPTION, Etc.

Age, 45 years; Height, 5ft. 6in.; sallow complexion; hair brown, turning grey; beard and moustache also turning grey, cropped close; square, stout build; nose slightly turned up; slouching gait, drops at the knees when walking, and turns his toes out. Speaks quickly and volubly, but not as an educated man. Generally dresses untidily for a man in his position, and has the appearance of a farmer.

When last seen was wearing a navy blue suit, motor cap, turned back, with buttons. Is an expert motorist.

Left Coventry at 2-20 on 28th inst.

It is urgently requested that search and enquiry be made at Hotels, Shipping Offices, and other likely places, and any information obtained should be immediately forwarded to the undersigned.

CITY POLICE OFFICE,
COVENTRY, 30th AUGUST, 1905.   **C. C. CHARSLEY.**

ILIFFE & SONS Limited, COVENTRY AND LONDON.

The Times, *6 November, 1922.*

TWO BANK CLERKS SHOT DEAD.

SEQUEL TO A QUARREL.

Two members of the staff of Messrs. Henry S. King and Co., bankers Pall-mall, Mr. Lindsay Lindsay, chief cashier, and Mr. Archie Gray, a clerk, were shot dead at the bank on Saturday, shortly after the premises had been closed to the public for the day.

The affair is believed to be the outcome of rivalry between the two men concerning a young woman employed at the bank as a typist, Miss Edith Ferguson. Shortly before half-past 1, Lindsay went to the basement to wash before leaving for the day, and was followed shortly afterwards by Gray. Other members of the staff heard the sounds of a heated argument followed by two revolver shots. Running to the basement, they found both men lying on the floor with wounds in the head. Gray was dead, and Lindsay died in a few minutes. The indications were that Lindsay had fired a revolver at Gray, and had then shot himself. Lindsay, it is understood, had a family bereavement not long ago, and an official at the bank told a Press representative that since that time he had appeared preoccupied and worried.

Miss Ferguson, who is 19, is the daughter of a police pensioner living at Carshalton. Her mother told a Press representative yesterday that she knew nothing about Lindsay except that her daughter had complained of his unwelcome attentions. Three months ago he called at the house and asked to see Miss Ferguson, and was told definitely that it was useless to continue his attentions. Gray and her daughter had been friends for years. They were both members of the Sutton Amateur Dramatic Society, and were to have taken part in a performance by the society in a week or two.

Staff of Regent Street, Clifton branch, 1925/6, pictured inside the branch. Bank staff held a respected, as well as respectable, position in local society. They often acted as treasurers to local clubs and charities. Instructions were issued from Head Office Staff Department on the standard of dress expected of staff. For work clerks were told to wear a black coat and waistcoat, grey striped trousers, white shirt with stiff linen collar, dark tie, bowler hat and rolled umbrella.

In 1929, for the first time, six girls were appointed to the staff of Accounts Department, 39 Threadneedle Street. The girls were there for the express purpose of mechanising the branch. They became known as the 'Tiller Girls' because they worked the tills. Ledgers were done on Burroughs machines and later the whole process was done by National Machine. Pictured on the roof of 39 Threadneedle Street in the early 1940's are these ledger girls. They all wore navy blue alpaca overalls, supplied by the Bank, to save their own clothing. All the women were single, for until 1949 any women on the permanent staff who married had to resign.

When the girls were appointed to the staff it was later reported by the The Dark Horse *that they were received with some hostility by the male members of staff who feared their positions were in jeopardy. Although at first they did exactly the same work as men, writing up passbooks, they were there for the express purpose of mechanising the branch. After training in the use of machines by Remingtons they did the waste and typed the statements and were eventually accepted by the men.*

R. W. Ellis wrote to the magazine to correct the report:

'Eight months before the girls arrived we were told that we were to be afforded the dubious privilege of becoming the first mechanised branch. Mr Bunster and his mechanisation staff descended upon us and six machines appeared in the centre of the office. I remember that it was a superstition among the staff never to approach too close to the machines or evince too much interest for fear of being roped in.

For six months we men operated the machines, to our disgust, for we had been promised lady operators. When the great day came, and six demure young misses arrived, they were as welcome as the flowers in spring. If we men seemed distant in our greetings it was because we had been briefed not to fraternise too enthusiastically, and it was a strain amending our vocabulary now that there were ladies present! If there was any hostility from the men it was against the Bank for making the girls wear those awful overalls!'

J. M. T. Wallace, Foreign Exchange Dealer, at work 1920, in the offices of Cox & Co, 16 Charing Cross, London. This dealer could deal in pounds worth then $4.86. Note the four candlestick telephones on pergolas or lazy-tongs.

Messenger staff, about 1932–36, at Colonial & Foreign Dept, Gracechurch Street, wearing top hats.

Corn Street, Bristol branch, about 1928. Back row: Messrs Plaskett, Rugman, Wall, Deft, Linney, Pollard, Martin, Clarke, Tidmarsh, Yeoman, Youngson. Second row: Dyke, Lawton (Messenger), Wade, Collier, Everett, Salter, Sawtell, Reynolds, Dickens, Brown, Henderson, Norris, Stokes, Walker, Freeman, Street (Messenger), J. W. Hamilton-Roberts. Seated: Jenkins, Lavington, Miss Jakeman, Mrs Godwin, S. W. Viveash (Assistant Manager), H. G. Treasure (Manager), H. F. Banner (Assistant Manager), Miss Miller, Miss Cowgill. Seated on floor: Grieves, White, Thomas, Pryce, Molyneux (?), Rudge, Pinney.

Staff at work, Corn Street, Bristol branch, about 1928.

Staff at work inside Sheffield branch, about 1929. Pictured are cashiers: Walter Wildblood, R. C. 'Willie' Williamson (an early wireless buff), Brian Pringle, E. G. Teare (later to become a signatory on the Isle of Man banknotes). On the desk behind are: Alfred Rowley (securities), Philip Brunton (ledgers), ?, E. D. Eastick (who later left the bank to become a stamp dealer) and Bill Fish. On the desk with the book-rails is Rex Collins, who died on active service in Italy.

Staff at work behind the counter of Gooch Street, Birmingham about 1930. (Notice states: Foreign Business Transacted, World Letters of Credit & Travellers Cheques Issued, Savings Bank Accounts Opened, Home Safes Issued, Executorships & Trusteeships Undertaken.) The gentleman in the centre is the Manager, George Leonard Teare.

BANK FIGHT: *Lloyds' Chairman makes Bold Move to Defeat Bank Employees' Organisation After Stern Battle over Workers' Rights*

PLANTING himself at the head of a long table in the wooden-panelled board room of Lloyds Bank's imposing Lombard-street head office, the Bank's chairman, walrus-moustached James Beaumont Pease, three weeks ago, faced his 34 fellow-directors. Indignantly asserting he would brook no further interference from the Bank Officers' Guild, progressive organisation of bank clerks, he ordered an extraordinary general meeting of his shareholders for Friday, July 17.

Regarded as one of the banking events of the year, the meeting has nevertheless found little publicity in the City of London. With one sweep, Chairman Beaumont Pease, now choosing a title for the barony conferred on him in the recent Birthday Honours, plans to put the black-coated workers in their place, and to entrench Lloyds Bank board firmly against small shareholders.

Chief champion of the lowly bank employee is 37-year-old Secretary Thomas Gilbert Edwards, of the Bank Officers' Guild, now 20,000 strong, who has been spending a holiday at Beltinge, Kent, preparing a scheme to frustrate the shrewd banker's withering attack.

Well-known in the banking community as a vigorous opponent of Banker Beaumont Pease, T. G. Edwards threw up his job as Branch Accountant with the National Provincial Bank in June, 1934, to lead the Guild, formed in 1918 to safeguard the interests of bank employees, and to raise the standard of "professional behaviour."

A Bitter Attack

Charging Lloyds with having made more drastic cuts in staff remuneration than other British banks, the Guild hopefully tabled several resolutions for last January's annual meeting of the Bank, including one which bitterly invited shareholders to decide:

"That having regard to the fact that for many years past it has been recognised by responsible employers, including the Government in its capacity of employer, that it is fair and proper that independent employees' associations shall be recognised for the purposes of discussion and consideration of the conditions of employment of staffs, this meeting regrets the policy of the bank in refusing recognition of the Bank Officers' Guild, and is of opinion that such refusal is not in accord with what is now widely recognised as fair and proper, and considers such a refusal to be prejudicial to the best interest of the bank."

Several shareholders protested · against the agenda. Others sat back to enjoy the rare experience of a squabble at a dignified bank meeting. Chairman Beaumont Pease tolerantly called for a fair

Chairman Beaumont Pease
... putting the black-coated workers in their place

hearing, himself suggesting a "full and frank discussion."

Into the employees' camp he boldly carried the battle, disclosing:

"Some months ago I anticipated that some such resolution would be brought up. . . . We had noticed the transfers of various single shares being made into the names of about 20 individuals, subsequently rising to 41, most of them giving as their address the headquarters of the Bank Officers' Guild. . . . It seemed fairly obvious that these single shares were being bought with the object of qualifying as shareholders in order to propose and support some such resolution. . . . All the resolutions following the ordinary agenda have been sent in by shareholders possessing one share each." Put to the meeting, the Guild's first resolution was swamped.

Guild Secretary T. G. Edwards
... "We are undismayed"

Basis of the Chairman's opposition to the Guild was that Lloyds Bank already maintains its own Staff Representative Committee to look after workers' interests.

Before the Guild could face the meeting with its other resolutions, Sir Arthur Sutherland, Newcastle shareholder, rose to stop discussion, called the whole affair "an abuse of the provisions of the Articles of Association," moved that the meeting be closed, and carried the day amid protests from outwitted Guild representatives.

New Rules

That Mr. Beaumont Pease also considered the Guild's attack an abuse of the Bank's Articles is now clear from his decision to propose an alteration at next week's meeting.

Under existing rules, shareholders are entitled to submit resolutions at General Meetings. New rules proposed by the Directors forbid any shareholder moving any resolution at General Meetings—an almost unheard-of innovation in the conservative City of London.

If Chairman Beaumont Pease has his way at the meeting, a poll may be demanded by shareholders possessing not fewer than 10,000 shares; old rule: a poll could be demanded by members holding 500 shares.

No detailed copies of these revolutionary proposals have been circulated to shareholders, who are blandly told that copies are available for inspection, or can be had on application.

This week, small shareholders who don't much mind whether the Bank Officers' Guild wins or loses its struggle, were beginning to realise that through Chairman Beaumont Pease's wily counter-move, their own rights will dwindle, that more power will pass to the Directors. Returning from holiday, Guild Secretary Edwards declared: "We are undismayed."

News Review, 9 July 1936. The Bank Officers Guild was started in 1918 to form a new 'combination of bank clerks'. In 1946 it became the National Union of Bank Employees. Today, it is known as the Banking Insurance and Finance Union (BIFU).

'Clerk-in-Charge' branch at West Bowling, Bradford, about 1960. Inside the branch are pictured R. Kipling and Malcolm Crane with a junior clerk in the background. Note the pewter inkpot on the counter. The clerks standing outside the branch include Malcolm Crane and Bill Roberts (Clerk-in-Charge).

Bernard Smith of Aylesbury Overseas branch with Chris Pinnock on his knee surrounded by colleagues Anna Palinski, Jane Franklin, Kim Farrell, Wendy Wilson, Sue Duval and Jennie Hawkins. Bernard was nominated by his colleagues as someone special who deserved a special 'thank-you' in the 1980 Lloyds Bank News 'Personality-Plus' competition. The ultimate winner of the competition was Mrs Irene Fish of Data Processing Operations Department.

Alan Wilkinson, pictured December 1986, outside Hindhead Training Centre on his retirement after 36 years service. Alan was engaged as PT instructor in 1950 and many former course-members will remember his orienteering tests. He also organised the gymnastics display for the Bank's Sports Day at Beckenham for many years and was full-time secretary of the Bank's Sailing Club.

Carole Moakes, Bank Relations, pictured in July 1987 as the Bank's first lady messenger to be employed in the City of London. Before becoming a messenger four months previously, she worked as a Lloyds Bank Cleaner at 6 Eastcheap. Carole told Lloyds Bank News: *'I joined the Messenger staff for a change and to improve my position in the bank. I enjoy working with all my colleagues – they're a smashing bunch of lads!'*

October 1987, Staff Suggestion Scheme winner, Roger Barette, won £2,000 for writing a computer program which among other things produces and prints dividend, tax and commission vouchers, and a report for records. The saving to his branch in Jersey has been about three staff, which is valuable as staff are not so easy to find as on the mainland.

Training

In 1966 a two-tier recruitment system was started and with it came changes in the training systems that had been set up after the War. Previously all youngsters joining the Bank had started with equal status and opportunity. Training consisted of being taught by another clerk and this became known as 'sitting by Nellie'. A small number of potential managers and officials were now given accelerated training.

On the job training was supplemented in 1968 by 'programmed learning' courses which were introduced into the branches. These were originally developed in the USA. The courses were specially written at Hindhead and covered aspects of branch work which young clerks could study on their own for an hour a day.

Having completed these courses clerks went on a Preliminary Course at the training centre at Hindhead which lasted several weeks and covered the elements of branch banking. As the young recruit developed his or her knowledge, courses on lending and security work and junior management followed. Finally a Senior Course was taken at the Staff College, Eyhurst Court, Kingswood and, for a select few, a course at the Administrative Staff College at Henley or one of the business schools.

The Beacon Hotel, Hindhead, pre-1914. The hotel was bought by Lloyds Bank for £32,500 with a further £24,270 being spent on repairs and alterations. The first course in October 1950 lasted eight weeks under the guidance of the principal R. J. Blanch and his 12 instructors. New entrants to the bank were given basic training in junior work and those considered unsuitable for work in the Bank were soon weeded out.

Second Junior Course, 1950. Staff College, which produced a good crop of Regional General Managers. Some of the people pictured are John R. Jones, Alan Osborne, K. Sinclair and D. W. Kendrick.

Lloyds Bank Staff College, Fifth Junior Course, 4 January – 22 February 1952

Back row: A. Turner, (Leeds); R. L. Blackmore, (Albert Road, Southsea); S. G. R. Morgan, (Cirencester); L. A. S. Spong, (Cheapside, EC2); J. A. Hobby, (Freshwater, IoW); N. E. Rogers, (Temple Row, Birmingham); D. W. Bowen, (Newnham, Glos); I. S. Luscombe, (Bridgwater); L. F. Hudson, (Gants Hill, Ilford); H. Rees-Mathews, (Whitchurch, Shrops); W. F. Brookes, (Corporation Street, Birmingham); R. H. Morgan, (Windsor); E. P. Banfield, (Camborne).
Third row: D. R. Hateley, (Regent Street, W1); E. G. Simpson, (Pall Mall, SW1); D. K. Hicks, (Newton Abbot); F. J. Green, (Yeovil); H. A. Barratt, (Law Courts, WC2); N. W. Jones, (Stock Exchange, EC2); R. J. K. Ellis, (Blandford); G. H. Basnett, (New Street, Birmingham); L. B. Nichols, (Southend-on-Sea); J. H. M. Walker, (Maidstone, Kent); K. A. Slater, (Bexhill-on-Sea).
Second row: F. N. Coomber, (Cullompton); A. J. Scholefield, (Cardiff); L. G. Lale, (Pitsea); A. V. Taylor, (Charing Cross, Birkenhead); K. A. Durden, (Piccadilly, W1); J. S. Ellis, (Collingwood Street, Newcastle); T. W. Aplin, (Cambridge); W. F. Le Page, (Worcester Park); A. D. C. McKie, (Worcester); F. A. Ford, (St James's Street, SW1).
Front row: J. D. Crawshaw, (Selby); R. E. A. Foulger, (Bursar); F. O. Jefferson, (Instructor); W. E. Roach, (Instructor); W. B. Fowler, (Senior Instructor); W. Murgatroyd, (Principal); F. T. Thew, (Instructor); E. Everest, (Instructor); J. C. Toope, (Instructor); G. R. Kinsey, (Assistant Instructor); M. F. J. Schyns, (Kilburn and Brondesbury, NW6).

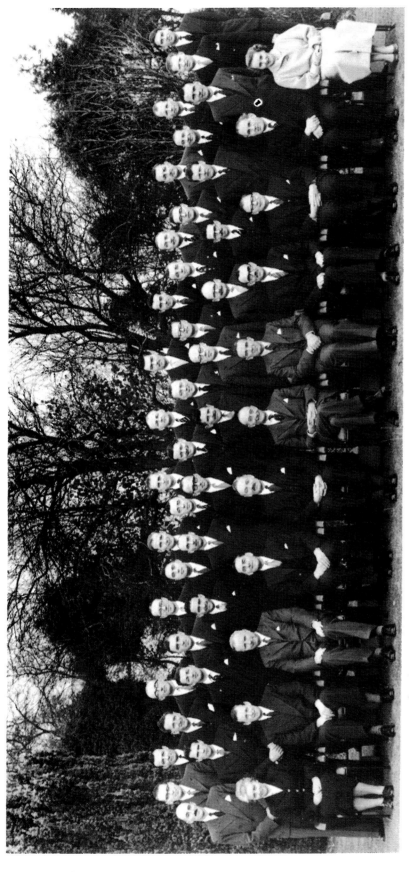

Lloyds Bank Staff College, Twenty-first Senior Course, 14 November 1955 – 13 January 1956

Back row: R. J. Barker, (Tonbridge); S. P. Pegrum, (Harehills); F. E. Kingdon, (Leadenhall Street, EC3); J. A. Nurse, (Westminster House, SW1); J. A. Richardson, (Harrogate); S. Copplestone, (Liverpool); D. H. Davies, (Inspector's Assistant); J. D. Smart, (Inspector's Assistant); B. P. Tebbutt, (E & T Dept, Exeter); W. H. Naylor, (Newark); R. H. Morgan, (Newbury); R. L. Blackmore, (Inspector's Assistant).

Third row: S. W. Howe, (Chopwell); W. F. Brookes, (Dudley); T. H. F. Creed, (Cullompton); A. W. Goodman, (Inspector's Assistant); J. E. D. Lockyer, (Inspector's Assistant); G. H. Priddle, (Bishop's Stortford); G. H. Basnett, (New Street, Birmingham); F. W. Crawley, (Inspector's Assistant); D. E. Scott, (Inspector's Assistant); J. D. Pipkin, (Sleaford); C. G. Smith, (Minehead); V. F. C. Tyrrell, (Inspector's Assistant).

Second row: D. J. Moore, (Swansea); F. Waldie, (Inspector's Assistant); H. A. Pearse, (Inspector's Assistant); F. J. Green, (Wiveliscombe); G. D. Jaggers, (Pall Mall, SW1); K. A. Slater, (Silverhill); T. E. Edward, (HO, Unattached); H. M. M. Wale, (Inspector's Assistant); J. R. Jones, (Crickhowell); J. W. Bateman, (Stafford); W. A. H. Weston, (West Southbourne); J. C. Williams, (Cheltenham Road, Bristol).

Front row: Miss D. Belcher; P. Rayner, (Assistant Instructor); E. J. Furley, (Instructor); C. R. Daniels, (Instructor); J. G. C. Toope, (Senior Instructor); R. K. Spencer, (Principal); E. Hirst, (Instructor); W. N. Spall, (Instructor); A. L. Dawson, (Instructor); P. B. Collings, (Bursar's Assistant); Miss M. Greengrass.

Lloyds Bank Training Centre, Preliminary Course No 31, 1 June – 3 July 1970

Back row: D. Eastham, (Preston); C. J. Walker, (Gateshead); A. F. Cooper, (Maidstone); R. H. Clarke, (Portswood); P. J. Kelly (Great Portland Street); A. P. Bevington, (Totterdown); D. C. Champion, (Hawarden); B. Williams, (Truro); J. A. Grayson, (Newport, Mon); R. M. Blakey, (Small Heath).

Fifth row: F. G. Hawkins, (Carters Green); R. E. Hutchings-Webber, (Budleigh Salterton); P. Saint, (The Moor); R. M. Way, (Ascot); L. T. McIlroy, (Andover); D. M. Shilling, (Baker Street); R. C. Southerden, (Lansdowne); M. E. Cantwell, (Swindon); M. L. V. Dale, (Charing Cross); A. T. Kerr, (Tetbury); R. Lawrenson, (Redcar); D. C. Pugsley, (Bridgwater).

Fourth row: S. Rhodes, (Cannon Street); Author, (Dunstable); J. R. Mackie, (Chippenham); R. Richards, (Wednesbury); R. J. Maynard, (Pontypridd); A. Robinson, (Scarborough); D. J. Willshire, (Fareham); P. W. Dacombe, (Dorchester); B. L. King, (West Smithfield); M. H. Grover, (Market, Swansea); C. T. Loughlin, (Cheltenham); D. F. H. Dew, (Hereford); C. A. G. Pryor, (Colchester).

Third row: W. S. Stanley, (Moreton-in-Marsh); S. P. Anderson, (Bradford); B. D. Thomas, (Poole); R. Mander, (Brockenhurst); I. G. A. McDonald, (Christchurch); P. J. Healey, (Liverpool); J. W. Ritchie, (Harpenden); J. Dixon, (Regent Street); S. D. Wadman, (Shoreham-by-Sea); M. C. Hopkins, (Rochester); P. H. Nunnerley, (Mincing Lane); M. A. Nicholas, (Sussex Place); P. E. Clapp, (Exeter); G. J. Webster, (Hunslet).

Second row: R. Isaac, (Minehead); T. A. Bowler, (Blackpool); C. A. L. Illidge, (Hull); R. A. L. Davies, (Kingsway); K. H. Rostron, (Durham); R. A. Wicks, (Bayswater); R. G. Bickmore, (Reigate); J. P. Freebairn, (Gosforth); A. J. Grout, (Earlsdon); J. R. Gout, (Marble Arch); J. M. Cousins, (Cambridge); M. N. Taylor, (Wembley); N. Wolfenden, (399 Oxford Street); J. D. T. Lewis, (Wind Street); M. J. R. Smardon, (Avonmouth).

First row: Mr I. R. Gillham (Branch Instructor); Mr J. O. Kerley, (Branch Instructor); Mr P. E. Smith, (Branch Instructor); Mr J. P. Windsor, (Branch Instructor); Mr J. R. Whalley, (Branch Instructor); Mr J. B. Rowson, (Instructor); Mr R. H. Smith, (Principal); Mr K. G. Till, (Senior Instructor); Mr R. P. Higgins, (Branch Instructor); Mr P. Heath, (Branch Instructor); Mr P. G. Webster, (Branch Instructor); Mr A. Wilkinson, (PT Instructor).

Lloyds Bank Training Centre, Intermediate Course No 62, 31 August – 1 October 1976

Fifth row – standing: C. R. Evans, (Bull Ring); R. A. G. Sweet, (Colmore Row); K. H. Davis, (Southampton); J. T. Ryan, (Vicar Lane, Leeds); S. T. R. Glover, (Camberley); G. J. Edwards, (Head Office Unattached, Bristol).

Fourth row – standing: J. Roberts, (Alum Rock); J. Back, (Uxbridge); R. N. Bayliss, (Washwood Heath); D. R. Rees, (Tetbury); C. R. Mullins, (Weymouth); J. O. Edwards, (High Street, Newport, Gwent); A. R. C. Peel, (Bitterne); W. R. Greenoff, (Market Place, Reading); N. J. Lapwood, (Hadleigh, Suffolk).

Third row – standing: C. L. Ayre, (Northampton); A. E. Smith, (Rye); G. W. Allen, (Minories); B. C. Mursell, (Maidenhead); D. E. Altoft, (Leicester); C. F. Evans, (Manchester); D. P. Hinton, (Tunbridge Wells); C. P. Vinnicombe, (Northwood); R. F. Lander, (Guildford); A. Allan, (Aldwych).

Second row – standing: A. P. Dean, (Fulwell); T. G. Phillips, (Chelsea); F. N. M. Brambell, (Cinderford); J. Adams, (York); R. J. H. Dossett, (Highcliffe-on-Sea); N. W. Smith, (Baker Street); D. Tallantyre, (Hexham); H. A. Pinner, (Exeter); G. Pope (Colchester); P. A. Smith, (Commercial Road, Portsmouth); M. E. May, (Truro).

Front row – seated: Mr D. G. Knapp, (Instructor); Mr D. N. Ablett, (Instructor); Mr J. P. White, (Instructor); Mr A. Gordon, (Senior Instructor); Mr S. R. Briggs, (Principal); Mr H. C. Bingham, (Instructor); Mr E. E. L. King, (Instructor); Mr D. N. Whalley, (Instructor).

Lloyds Bank Staff College, 136th Senior Course, 26 April 1982 – 28 May 1982

Back row: M. J. Burgess, (Inspector's Assistant, Leeds); R. B. Tullo, (Inspector's Assistant, London); I. D. Stevenson, (Norwich Trust); J. Roberts, (Inspector's Assistant, London); P. Aviss, (Inspector's Assistant, O & M Research Department); C. H. Cook, (Grindlays Bank Limited).
Third row: M. L. Ashdown, (Rainham); A. W. Reynolds, (Small Heath, Birmingham); E. A. Wiles, (Chiswick); R. N. Bayliss, (Inspector's Assistant, Nottingham); B. D. Thomas, (Cowes); D. K. Whalley, (Coventry); P. Niven, (Public Relations Department); R. E. Walrond, (Inspector's Assistant, Newcastle).
Second row: G. E. Parker, (Watford Trust); P. Burrows, (Inspector's Assistant, O & M Operations Department); D. W. Stokes, (Overseas Centre, Birmingham); S. Brooks, (Colchester); K. N. Lord, (Above Hill, Lincoln); H. A. Pinner, (Inspector's Assistant, O & M Research Department); P. Hale, Regent Street, Clifton).
Front row: Mr A. J. Budgett, (Bursar); Mr J. Ward, (Instructor); Mr J. A. Banks, (Deputy Principal); Mr J. J. Haworth, (Principal); Mr J. P. Salkeld, (Senior Instructor); Mr T. H. Waymouth, (Instructor); Mr M. V. Edwards. (Instructor); Miss C. H. Hill, (House Manageress).

First Overseas Division Advanced Development Course, Training Centre, Hindhead, 23 March – 3 April 1981. Pictured are: (back row) Tony Bull, (Overseas Centre, Birmingham); John Bird, (Instructor); Author; (middle row) Graham Carter, (Overseas Branch, Leicester); Bryan McNeil, (Overseas, Newcastle); Bob Evans, (Overseas Division, London); Malcolm MacBeth, (Overseas Centre, Birmingham); (front row) Neil Bradley, (Overseas Centre, Birmingham); Susan Hutton-Ashkenny, (Overseas Branch, Maidstone); Dennis Le Queux, (Training Section); John Dorrell, (Training Section); Audrey Brown, (Overseas Branch, Bristol); Cambell McElveen, (Overseas Division, London).

Pictured in 1985, 25 years on, the 'young men with potential' who attended the 33rd Senior Course still gather for regular weekend reunions. Back row: Ian Brodie, Chief Manager (International), Overseas Division; John Burnell, Manager, Regent Street; Jack Dodgeon, retired Manager, Piccadilly, Manchester; and Harry Robin, retired Manager, Bournemouth.
Middle row: George Walker, retired RSM, South Wales; John Luce, Deputy Manager, Pall Mall; Cyril Hardy, Manager, Bradford; Brian Pitman, Group Chief Executive and Austen Townsend, Manager, Vicar Lane.
Front row: Graham Bliss, retired Manager, Edgbaston; Eric Willis, Manager, Slough; Ray Gregory, retired Manager, Newton Abbot; Ken Barber, Chief Manager, Export Finance Division; Len Dalliamore, retired Manager, Cwmbran; Gordon Parker, retired Manager, Temple Row; David James, retired Manager, Wrexham and Vic Rawley, Assistant Chief Manager, Export Finance Division.

Sporting Activities

Cycle run to Southwell, 21 June 1904. The staff of Bridlesmith Gate, Nottingham branch photographed outside the Cathedral before a cycle run to Southwell. Pictured standing: S. J. T. Eacott, (Alfreton Road branch); F. R. Hole, W. Merchant, W. E. Hemming, W. E. Holbrook, E. R. Oliver, G. G. Gadd, E. H. Wilson. Seated: O. E. Walker, G. S. Allcock.

Beehive Sports Club, winners – 'Montague Turner' Bowls Challenge Cup, 1934. Standing: Mr Copps, A. E. Redman, S. Drew, E. J. Stocks, G. H. Lipscombe. Sitting: W. Batchelor (Vice Captain); T. Tuck, W. G. Edwards, (Chairman); J. G. B. Orbell, (Honorary Secretary); J. Chandler, (Captain).

Lloyds Bank London XI Football Continental Tour, Easter 1928. The picture was taken at the YMCA, on the coast road outside Boulogne. Not all of the group who went on the tour are pictured. Members of the Bank's football club who went included: Bob Burges, Frank Crang, Cuthbert Hughes, Curly Collins, Mike Hunt, George Carle, Harry Oldershaw, Freddie Stiff, Jock Campbell, Gordon Aucott, Steve Stephenson, Steve Ash, Tom Ralph (groundsman at the Bank's sports club, Beckenham), Frank Stone, Frank Jones, Don and Ernie Gow.

Staff at Dark Horse Sports Club, Lahore, 29 July 1941, enjoying a swim, followed by a dinner. Maurice Kershaw and Bob Osborn were present.

Lloyds Bank Association Football Club. London v Country, 5 March 1977. Result 2–2.

Back row: D. M. Sweeney (Knightsbridge), Secretary; P. Dickeson, (Catford) Referee; D. Godfrey, (Head Office) Assistant Coach; M. Harkess, (Guildford Trust); R. Entwistle, (Wigmore Street); R. Evans, (Rhos-on-Sea); A. Brown, (Guildford); C. M. Teare (O & M Res); C. Collier, (O & M Res); R. Sharpe, (DPOD); D. Edwards, (Leigh Park); R. Bishop, (Headington), Linesman; E. Clarke, (Guildford) Country Selector.
Middle row: P. Foster, (DPOD); J. Rowlands, (Blackburn); T. Boatwright, (Cheque Clg); M. Lockyer, (Chief Ins) County Captain; N. J. Coy, (Sheffield) County Selector; G. W. Blick, (Chairman) London FC; V. F. Tyrrell, (Chairman) Sports Club; N. Blick, (City Office) Town Captain; W. Race, (Rotherham); R. Berry, Town Coach.
Front row: S. Kaplanski, (Newington Causeway); D. Tattersall, (Blackburn); J. O'Donnell, (Curzon Street); J. Roberts, (O & M Res); M. Dyett, (399 Oxford Street); J. Blackmore, (Abingdon); R. Morgan, (Law Courts); S. Hyde, (Marlborough); A. Matthews, (DPD); R. Gawne, (Grantham).

Lloyds Bank Association Football Club. London v Country, 3 March 1979. Result 2–4.

Back row: M. Webster, (Linesman); A. Mitchell, (Liskeard); M. Dyet, (399 Oxford Street); B. M. Jones, (Corporation Street, Coventry); D. Williams, (Moorgate); G. T. Veale, (Aberdare); E. Fraser, (Cheque Clearing); S. Lewis, (Sussex Place, Bristol); A. Care, (Willenhall); R. Bishop, (Linesman).
Middle row: M. Harkess, (Guildford Trust); S. Kaplanski, (Kentish Town); P. Breach, (Carterton); T. Allan, (Kentish Town); S. G. Cook, (Cirencester); K. Norbury, (DPOD); R. Gawne, (Borough Road, Burton-on-Trent); D. Rouse, (DPOD); A. D. Wingrove, (Referee).
Seated: J. H. Green, (Chesterfield); P. Foster, (DPOD) Town Captain; N. J. Coy, (Country Selector); G. W. Blick, (Chairman); E. J. Clarke, (Country Selector); N. Purcell, (Hon Secretary); C. J. Parsons, (Stroud), Country Captain; G. Lockwood, (Wigmore Street).
Kneeling: P. Corbet, (Guernsey); J. Roberts, (O & M Research Department); J. Cavalli, (DPOD); K. C. Johnson, (Corporation Street, Coventry).

International Banking Division Running Team, 17 July 1986, taking part in a three-and-a-half mile run around the City of London course in the first Manufacturers Hanover Corporate Challenge. The race was limited to 2,000 competitors, but IBD were well represented, with 80 runners accounting for nearly 10 per cent of the Division's London-based staff.

The fastest individual times from the Division were from Jeff Claridge (20 minutes, 14 seconds) and for the ladies, Gail Johnson (27 minutes, 3 seconds). Some of the other runners pictured are: Peter Griffiths, Alan Ketley, Adrian Smith, Glyn Parlane, Gavin Kidman, Chris Oram, Jim Leonard, Andrew Budd, Tony Morgan, Steve Hyams, David Hill, Ivan Hilton, Jackie Chapman, Jackie Dupouy, Sheri Barratt, Alistair Caie, Barry Heaton, John Dreuce, Bob Miskin, Carl Lange, Dave Skelton, Paul Starling, Peter Burroughs, Terry Wood, Dave Edwards, Andy Hunt, Bob Parsons, Adrian Tooth, Kevin Hall, Chris Clarke, Jackie Mitchelmore, Sheila Clapham, Teresa Barnes, Heather Wheeller, David Oakley and Andrew Kirby.

First meeting of the Lloyds Bank National Ladies Golf Society 1989. The three-day gathering took place at Tewkesbury Park and was attended by 27 lady golfers. The winner of the Lloyds Bank trophy was Meriel Barker (BHA – Gascoigne-Pees, Cobham).

Bank Celebrations

口———— T O A S T S ————口

ɔ

His Majesty The King

Proposed by ... ... THE CHAIRMAN

The Chairman

Proposed by ... ... H. C. CROFTON, Esq.

The Colonial and Foreign Department

Proposed by ... ... H. S. CARTER, Esq.
Reply by ... ...

ɔ

PROGRAMME OF CONCERT

1. Miss HILDA BERTRAM ... Songs at the Piano

2. Mr. H. J. JUPP—
   " Wimmen, Oh ! Wimmen ! " ... *Phillips*
   " Rolling down to Rio " ... ... *German*

3. Mr. H. W. BUDDEN—
   " I tried to keep from laughing "... ...

4. Mr. LLOYD HUWS—
   " A Corner of Cathoy " ... ... *Russell*
   " Soft little velvet eyes " ... ... *Meale*

5. Mr. A. E. SALMON—
   Recitations from his Repertoire

6. Mr. A. R. COLE—
   " The Mistress of the Master " ... *Phillips*
   " The Song of the Waggoner " *Breville-Smith*

7. Mr. CHARLES HARRIS (Humorist)

At the Piano—Mr. JOHN EDGAR

First Annual Dinner and Concert of the Colonial and Foreign Department, 17 Cornhill, held at the Café Monico, Piccadilly Circus, Monday, 21 November 1921. The chairman for the evening was W. Clifton Mould and the stewards were Dick Blore, Joe Busby, King Cole, Kris Lidwell and Paiday Snell.

Lloyds Bank Limited,
Guildford, Surrey.

Christmas
1940

New Year
1941

We, the undersigned members of the Staff of Lloyds Bank Limited, Guildford (hereinafter called <u>the</u> Staff) do hereby send Cordial Greetings to our erstwhile Colleagues, AND by our act and deed do signify our remembrance of you jointly and severally.

Wartime Christmas card from Guildford branch sent to their 'erstwhile colleagues', Christmas 1940. The previous Christmas, the Rifle Section sent their own Christmas message in The Dark Horse *magazine: 'We take this opportunity to extend our Christmas greetings to all our members in every branch of His Majesty's Services. To those who find themselves far away in the desert, chewing sand, in the Army, preparing for the Big Push, in the RAF, having all the fun, and in the Navy, doing extremely useful work, or at home, sitting all night in a warden's dug-out, waiting for an air-raid which seems a long while in coming. As far as we can see at present it does not appear too unreasonable to hope that this will be the only Christmas to be spent under war conditions. We are expecting great happenings in the New Year.'*

Annual Bank Dinner, about 1930. Note they were for the men only.

First Inspectors reunion, early 1950s.

Pall Mall branch, soon after dawn on Tuesday, 2 June 1953. A holiday for all the staff to celebrate the coronation of Queen Elizabeth II.

Some 40 television sets were installed in the branch for the day. Floral decorations were supplied by the Staff College.

LLOYDS BANK LIMITED

Cox's and King's Branch: 6, PALL MALL, S.W.1

Coronation—2nd June, 1953

MENU

BUFFETS ON ALL FLOORS WILL BE OPEN FROM 7.30 a.m. ONWARDS

Breakfast:

Grapefruit — Tomato juice

Hot:— Bacon & Sausage Roll
Scrambled Egg on Toast

Cold:— Scotch Egg — Pork Pie
Egg Sandwiches
Ham Sandwiches

Bridge Rolls & Butter

Marmalade — Jam — Honey

Dessert Fruit

Coffee   Tea

Morning Coffee and Biscuits

Luncheon:

Cocktail Savouries

Scotch Salmon Mayonnaise
Lobster Salad
Chicken Chaudfroid
Asparagus Rolls
Chicken vol-au-vent
Salmon, Prawn and Shrimp Patties
Stuffed Eggs

Potato Salad   Russian Salad
Lettuce & Tomato Salad

Sandwiches: Ham, Chicken, Tongue, Egg, Cheese, Tomato, Salmon, Smoked Salmon, Sardine, Beef and Lamb

Bridge Rolls: Assorted Fillings

Sweets: Strawberries & Cream — Raspberry Souffle — Individual Trifles — Meringues & Ice Cream — Jellied Fruits — Strawberry & Raspberry Tartlets — Fresh Fruit Salad

Sundaes:— Ice Cream   Choc. Ices

Cheese: Gorgonzola — Cheddar — Cream Cheese

French Bread — Rolls — Biscuits

Tea   Coffee

Tea:

Assorted Cakes and Pastries

Refreshments were available to the staff and their guests on all floors from 7.30 am onwards.

Aylesbury Overseas enter the local carnival, Summer 1973. Some of the people pictured include: Anna Palinski, John Owen, David Clear, Valerie Norfield, Hilary Rice, Wendy Cowley, Gordon Bishop, (Market Square, Aylesbury) and David Curtis.

Party, Leicester Overseas, 1974 on the occasion of Keith Hoon (left) Sub-Manager moving to Aylesbury Overseas as Assistant Manager. Also pictured are Phil Lilley (Assistant Manager) and Bob Ross (Manager).

Miss Lloyds Bank contestants, 1987, gathered at the Southampton Park Hotel for the finals of Miss Lloyds Bank 1988. Pictured from the left are: Clare Withington, (Bridgnorth); Andrea Jones, (Ellesmere); Rachel Hutchings, (Aylesbury); Sonia McCready, (Preston, Lancs); Karen Weigh, (Christchurch); Helen Hewitt, (Lye); Stephanie Booth, (Colmore Row); Justine Williams, (Kempston); Lucy Prince, (Havant) and Julie Ford, (Wind Street, Swansea). The eventual winner was 21-year-old cashier Karen Weigh from Christchurch branch who won £600 in cash and shopping vouchers.

Lloyd Bank Managers playing the game 'Enterprise', 1987. The game which is on sale to the public at £14.99, gives an insight into the problems, opportunities and disappointments of real-life business. The game was designed by Ken Young, Head of Management Studies at Watford College and was launched by Lloyds Bank and Shell Oil. At the launch Mr Young (left) pits his wits against Colin Fisher, until recently Assistant General Manager, UK Retail Banking (now General Manager, Information Technology Division); Don Good, Chief Manager, Business Advisory Department; Malcolm Dolphin, Corporate Manager, Corporate Banking Division and Sydney Shore, Assistant General Manager, Corporate Banking Division.

Sir Jeremy Morse, Chairman, cutting the cake when he formally opened Hay's Lane House, London on 3 September 1987. David Wickham, Head Chef, who was responsible for the special cake is also pictured.

Lest we forget . . . Deputy Chairman Sir John Hedley Greenborough (centre) laid a wreath at the Bank's war memorial in City Office banking hall on Armistice Day, 11 November 1988. Among those present were (from left) standard-bearer John Newton, Messenger at Black Horse House; Eric Baker, Secretary of Lloyds Bank (City) House branch, Royal British Legion; Gerry Solomon, (General Manager, Branch Banking Division) and the Rev John Evans, of St Michael's Church, Cornhill. Piper Archie MacMaster (Messenger, Moorgate branch) played a lament at the memorial before the simple but moving ceremony took place.

Retirement

It is perhaps not widely known that retirement lunches are held at Head Office. Henry Lloyd, who retired from Union Street, Torquay at the end of December 1979, sent this account of his Lombard Street lunch to *The Dark Horse* magazine:

'About a month before my retirement the manager of my branch handed me a letter and said "You have an invitation". It was from the General Manager (Personnel Division) inviting me to lunch at Head Office. The letter also stated that the Bank would meet all costs of travel and incidental expenses for myself, and a member of my family, including an overnight stay at any London hotel of my choice.

My wife and I discussed the kind invitation and debated where we should stay. We are not complete strangers to "The Big City", as we lived and worked in London for several years while I was in the Royal Navy. However, we had found it difficult in subsequent trips to adjust to the continual noise of traffic, and we recalled that we had enjoyed the quiet of a really first-class hotel, so we decided to stay again at the London Hilton as we had done in 1962.

We planned to drive up from Devon on the day before the lunch. The weather started to deteriorate with fog and icy roads and at one stage we thought we might have to change plans and go by rail, but all was well in the end and we had a pleasant drive, arriving at the hotel well before the evening rush.

Afternoon tea was in the garden setting of the patio, pre-dinner drinks were in the South Seas atmosphere of Trader Vic's Bar, and we enjoyed a leisurely dinner, superbly cooked, in the Roof Restaurant with its excellent views of the lights of London. We then spent a very happy evening together dancing and listening to the groups who seemed to change about every half-hour.

The following morning after breakfast we took a taxi to Lombard Street to make sure I knew exactly where Head Office was, and then enjoyed a stroll round the City. It was rather sad to see so many new high-rise office blocks dwarfing the fine old buildings like the Royal Exchange and the Bank of England.

At about 12.30 my wife left me for a shopping expedition to Knightsbridge and I entered Head Office for my lunch appointment. I was delighted to meet about 16 other newly-retired members of staff and I was particularly pleased to meet again Edwin Smith. We had originally met 11 years before when I attended a military exercise at Taunton, but had since lost contact.

The lunch and wine were excellent and Mr Cullum's short speech thanking us, the guests, for our loyal and conscientious service to the Bank was followed by a invitation to look round Head Office. I was particularly interested to have the opportunity to see the Board Room, before having to keep my rendezvous with my wife.

To meet the General Manager and the other officials who entertained us was indeed a pleasure, and I would like to thank all concerned for what I found to be a very relaxed, informal and courteous atmosphere at an occasion which I shall long remember.'

Retirement, May 1988, of Frank Goodson, Aylesbury branch. Frank had worked at the branch for over 35 years apart from a short break when he was based at Wendover. On the day that he left male members of staff turned up wearing braces, affectionately marking the fact that he had been known as the only man in the branch donning this particular item of apparel every day.

The Bank's oldest pensioner, Alec Donald, celebrating his 101st birthday in 1987. Alec joined the Bank in 1902 at Stamford branch (when it was part of Capital & Counties Bank) and retired as Manager, St Albans in 1947. Alec celebrated his birthday at the James Marshall Home in Harpenden with Harpenden branch Manager John Leeson (left), RSLO Maisie Hand (right) and David Vernon, Senior Manager, St Albans branch. Also pictured are Alec's daughter-in-law (centre, back) and staff from the Home.

Did You Know . . .?

Old Bank

In the booklet *John Parry Wilkins and The Old Bank* by Susan Loram, published by Lloyds Bank, the author relates how the Old Bank, Brecon, managed to keep the confidence of its customers during a crisis:

'One family story is that during a crisis, rumour said the Old Bank was shaky and many came to Brecon to demand their money. No-one was refused. But the farmers could not carry large sums of money around with them. Mr Fryer, opposite the Bank, was one of the most notable merchants in the town, so many took their money to him for safe keeping. Mr Fryer had no facilities to keep large sums of money, so having given his customers a receipt, the money was returned to Mr Wilkins (at the Old Bank), through the back door, for safe keeping.

Because no-one was refused funds, confidence in the Bank's ability to keep open returned. Those who had left money with Mr Fryer went to collect it. Mr Fryer sent to the Bank for the money – his assistants using the back doors of both buildings – and the money was returned to Mr Wilkins by his clients through the front door!'

Holidays

Managers wishing to be absent from the Bank on private affairs for more that half-a-day, or giving their clerks such leave, were expected to give previous notice to the General Manager. *(Rules for Branch Managers, 1874).*

Till Shortages

In 1885 an elderly cashier in Lombard Street was pensioned when a shortage appeared for the second time in his till. For three years he suffered deduction from his pension, in partial restitution.

Retirement

At 60 years of age all salaried officers of the Bank were at liberty to apply for permission to retire on a pension, if they had served not less than 20 years. They had no option of retirement – that was for the Directors to decide. *(General Rules and Instructions, 1902.)*

Maintaining Rule Books

Every member of the staff had to make himself fully acquainted with the contents of the rule book – as, of course, is the case today – and had to produce his personal copy to an Inspector when required to do so. *(Book of Rules edition of the General Use of all Members of Staff, 1908.)*

Specialised Departments

There were only two specialised departments in the Bank until shortly after the Second World War. These were for overseas transactions and for executor and trustee business. The Foreign Department which later became known as the Colonial and Foreign Department was established in 1898 with a handful of staff. In 1921 the Bank sent John Fea, for 'temporary service of six months', to New York. Here he dealt in foreign exchange and only later became a proper representative of the Bank, staying until he retired in 1954! In 1950 the name was changed to Overseas Department, reflecting the decline in the British Empire.

The Executor & Trustee Department started business in 1910, when a special clause was added to the memorandum of association of the Bank, but it was not until 1919 that a separate department was created at 39 Threadneedle Street. The first branch was opened in 1933 in the West End of London.

Masonic Lodges

There are three Masonic Lodges associated with Lloyds Bank. The oldest was formed in 1900 by officials of the Capital and Counties Bank and is now named the Beehive Lodge after the former crest of Lloyds Bank. There is also the Black Horse of Lombard Street Lodge formed in 1920, the first Master being Sir Richard Vassar-Smith who was at the time the Chairman of the Bank. In 1946 the Beehive Lodge was started in Cardiff for bank staff in that area.

Lavatory Accommodation

Lavatory accommodation for women staff during and after the First World War was often a problem, as this was the first time that women had worked in the bank. The problem was acute in the smaller offices like St Austell which in 1921 were told 'accommodation for the lady clerks should be found somewhere outside the bank'.

Joint General Manager

The title Joint General Manager was introduced in 1919 as a result of an article in an evening newspaper signed by Sir John Ferguson, the London manager of the National Bank of Scotland. He became one of Lloyds' general managers as the result of the acquisition of the National Bank of Scotland in 1918. When he signed his letter 'General Manager' this upset caused a directive to be issued by the Chairman, Vassar-Smith, that all the general managers except Bell (Director and General Manager) should sign in future as 'joint' general managers.

Book Machine

In the 1920s H. J. Bailey, during the early days of his banking career in the Secretary's Department, used to type the minutes for the Board into green leather backed Board Minute Books. The typewriter, known in the office as the 'book machine', did type direct into the bound books. The machine looked very much like the early typewriters but with no roller and was mounted on a desk/table about 4ft square. It was raised from the front by a hinge on the back to allow the book to be placed under it. The page to be typed upon was then placed on a thick metal plate and the machine lowered upon the page. The only difference from the action of an ordinary typewriter being that when the keyboard was struck the arms bearing the letters came down instead of up.

The Bank Colour

The Bank colour green was adopted in the early 1920s at the suggestion of Major R. C. Garton, a Director 1918–23. Major Garton was a keen yachtsman and his boat in Poole harbour was covered with tarpaulins dyed 'Willesden green'. The boat stood out well from all the other yachts and he was therefore able to pick out his boat easily. He persuaded the Premises Committee of the Bank to adopt green for the Lloyds Bank signs as they would be visible at a distance. Today a somewhat darker shade than Willesden green is now used.

Manager's Discretionary Limit

The manager's discretionary limit for granting an advance was £100 which was fixed in 1920. In 1943 the limit was raised to a minimum of £250.

Merle Oberon

One of the telephone operators at Calcutta in the 1920s was a Miss Estelle Thompson, who later became the famous film actress, Merle Oberon.

Bath Chair

In 1920 the Board Staff Committee approved the purchase of a bath chair for the use of staff who were suffering a temporary incapacity. It is not known how frequently it was used or what became of it.

Lloyds Bank Outside the UK

The first branches abroad that carried the name of Lloyds Bank Ltd were in India (and subsequently Pakistan and Bangladesh), Kashmir, together with one branch in Burma between 1923 and 1961 and in Egypt between 1923 and 1926. The Bank's business in the East was handed over to National and Grindlays Bank in 1961.

Vernon Watkins

Vernon Watkins joined the Bank in 1925 and achieved an international reputation as a poet. He started as a clerk at St Helens, Swansea where he remained until he retired in 1966. Having no aspirations for a career in finance, he concentrated on his poetry. When he died in 1967, he was among the few then being considered as a successor to John Masefield as Poet Laureate.

Basil Boothroyd

Basil Boothroyd was a writer, journalist and broadcaster. He joined the bank in 1927, working for some 10 years in a number of branches in East Anglia. He then became Assistant Editor of *The Dark Horse* magazine. During his time as assistant editor he invented the mythical Coggles Bend branch of the Bank of Good Hope under the chaotic management of Mr Pitkin. He resigned from the Bank in 1952 to become Assistant Editor of *Punch*, to which he had contributed for some years. He achieved national and international fame as a humorist. He died in 1988, aged 77.

Overtime

In 1927 it was noted that there had been an increase in the extra payments for balance work at some branches. Staff were warned: 'The clerk who, through errors by him, is the cause of much wasted time, should not himself receive an allowance in that particular connection'.

The Banking Profession

In 1929 parents were told that their son might have to live away from home. In this event they had to be prepared to supplement his bank pay during the first few years. The Bank told parents that their son should regard himself 'in the light of an articled pupil'.

Night Safes

Night safes were invented and patented by F. Pritchard, a member of staff and later Manager of Premises Department. With the aid of a Meccano model, Pritchard successfully demonstrated his invention to the General Managers and Board with the result that in 1929 night safes were first installed in branches. They are still in use today.

Adolf Hitler

When this country took on Adolf Hitler on 3 September 1939, the Bank issued Circular 482C the following day. It was brief and forthright. The message was headed COMPETITION BETWEEN BANKS and the complete message read: 'It is understood that this shall cease during the War period. Managers must act accordingly'.

Jersey Besieged

In May 1945, in Jersey, when German currency was called in, there was a rush to the bank to exchange reichsmarks into sterling. For six days long queues besieged the branch. It was necessary for the St John Ambulance Brigade to be present in order to provide first aid in the banking hall.

Marriage

The obligation on women staff members to resign from the Bank on marriage was removed only in 1949. Female members of the permanent staff who wished to continue in the Bank's service after marriage could do so without any change in their permanent status – but on the strict understanding that 'their terms and conditions of service will be precisely as those applicable to single women members of the permanent staff'.

Bank Cars

In 1984 John Osborne, Head Chauffeur, recalled the history of the Bank cars in a conversation with John Booker, Bank Archivist. Apparently the first car owned by the Bank was a 1939 Wolseley, bought in 1949 for Lord Balfour of Burleigh. He remembers driving round in the car with a crate of milk bottles filled with water to top up a leaking radiator. The car, which was kept in Chelsea Mews, was superseded in 1951 by a Rolls-Bentley, colour midnight blue. There then followed two Austin Princess cars, one of which was used by the Chairman Sir Oliver Franks and the other for his deputy. When Harald Peake became Chairman, being a Rolls-Royce director, he always had his own Rolls and brought his own chauffeur with him. It is interesting to note that it was not done for chauffeurs to serve successive chairmen and all (except Peake's) were recruited from among the messengers. Next followed Armstrong Siddeley Sapphires which were hired from Victor Brittain of Paddington. These were followed by six or seven Daimler limousines.

When Sir Eric Faulkner became Chairman in 1969 he dispensed with the Rolls and during the petrol crisis of the early 1970s the Bank used front-wheel drive 1300cc Wolseley Saloons. These were followed by three-litre Rovers, burgundy coloured and then 4.2 Daimlers. At one time the number plate LB A1 was purchased through an advert in the *Exchange and Mart*. However, the arrangement of the registration number on the plate caused persistent intervention by the police as they wanted the letters closer together. The number was eventually sold by the Bank.

Seoul Paralympics

Blind runner Bob Matthews, MBE, audio-typist from Personnel Division, won a gold medal in the 1988 Paralympics held at Seoul. With the aid of a guide he won the 5,000 metres for Great Britain.

Staff Suggestion Scheme

The Staff Suggestions Scheme payments in 1988 topped £37,150 – 85 per cent up on 1987, and a record. There were 183 awards to staff – averaging £203 per suggestion.

Lloyd's of London

There is no historical association between Lloyds Bank and Lloyd's of London. The use of the apostrophe distinguishes the shipping and insurance concern from Lloyds Bank.

Important Dates and Events

1677 Earliest known reference to the sign of the black horse in Lombard Street.

1765 Taylors and Lloyds founded in Birmingham.

1771 Hanbury, Taylor, Lloyd and Bowmans Bank opened in Lombard Street, London.

1865 Banking partnership dissolved – new joint stock company, Lloyds Banking Company Limited, formed.

1884 Merger with Barnetts, Hoares, Hanbury & Lloyd, whose·symbol was the black horse.

1900 Liverpool Union Bank taken over resulting in Lloyds Bank becoming established in Lancashire.

1911 Lloyds Bank (France) Ltd, Paris office opened.

1914 Wilts and Dorset Banking Company acquired.

1918 Capital and Counties merger, adding 473 offices.

1923 Substantial holding acquired in Bank of London & South America.

Cox & Co and Henry S. King & Co, banking agents for India, taken over.

1964 Lloyds Bank Europe Ltd established.

1965 Link with Mellon National Bank of Pittsburgh.

1966 The National Bank of New Zealand became a wholly-owned subsidiary.

1970 Lloyds Associated Banking Company (LABCO) set up.

1971 Merger of Lloyds Bank Europe and Bank of London & South America to form Lloyds & Bolsa International Bank.

Joint Credit Card Company formed which operates the Access credit card.

1972 Cashpoint introduced.

1973 All branches computerised.

1973/4 Lloyds Bank International established incorporating Bank of London & South America.

1979 Home Loan scheme launched, the first by a Clearing Bank.

1982 Black Horse Agencies launched to become the largest estate agency chain in the country.

1984 Schroder, Munchmeyer, Hengst of West Germany became a member of the Group.

1986 The businesses of Lloyds Bank Plc and Lloyds Bank International Ltd were merged on 1 January 1986.

Most of the business of the Continental Bank of Canada was bought.

1988 Lloyds Bowmaker Finance, Black Horse Agencies, Black Horse Life Assurance Company, Lloyds Bank Unit Trust Managers and Lloyds Bank Insurance Services merged with Abbey Life Group.

1989 First of the Big Four banks to pay interest on certain current accounts.

Staff List, 1 January 1903

DIRECTORS

J. Spencer Phillips, Esq, The Mount, Shrewsbury *(Chairman)*. Charles E. Barnett, Esq, Edgegrove, Watford, Herts. J. B. Close Brooks, Esq, Birtles Hall, Chelford, Cheshire. William de Winton, Esq, Maesderwen, Brecon. Herbert W. Hind, Esq, 2 Old Church Yard, Liverpool. E. Brodie Hoare, Esq, Tenchleys, Limpsfield, Surrey. Richard Hobson, Esq, 54 Brown's Buildings, Liverpool. J. Arthur Kenrick, Esq, Berrow Court, Edgbaston. George B. Lloyd, Esq, Edgbaston Grove, Church Road, Edgbaston. Howard Lloyd, Esq, Grafton Manor, Bromsgrove. Richard B. Lloyd, Esq, Fir Grove, Farnham, Surrey. Sir Thomas Salt, Bart, Weeping Cross, Stafford. William Small, Esq, Devon House, Leamington. A. W. Summers, Esq, Tellisford House, Clifton Down, Bristol. James Tomkinson, Esq, MP, Willington Hall, Tarporley, Cheshire. R. V. Vassar-Smith, Esq, Charlton Park, Cheltenham. George D. Whatman, Esq, 2 Cranley Gardens, South Kensington, SW. Robert Woodward, Esq, Arley Castle, Bewdley.

HEAD OFFICES
LONDON: 71 Lombard Street, EC

General Manager: E. Alexander Duff.

General Manager's Assistants: J. P. Benwell, C. E. Cobb.

Advance Department: D. Whyte, W. F. Massingham.

Chief Accountant: J. Frith.

Inspector for London District: W. W. Mitchell.

BIRMINGHAM: Edmund Street

Country General Managers: J. Dixon Taylor, Alexander Fyshe.

Chief Inspector: G. W. Baldwin.

Secretary: Edward J. Harrison.

Assistant Secretary: C. H. Bradbury.

Assistant Country Managers: C. P. Newman, Henry Bell.

Advance Department: S. Titterton, Herbert Gray.

Inspectors of Branches: George Tyler, W. J. Burden, A. Davidson, W. C. Buckley, A. V. Williams, A. G. Barker, John Counsell.

LONDON HEAD OFFICE

Staff – Advance Department: C. E. Appleby, E. M. Bray, G. L. Chambers.

General Manager's Private Secretary: G. J. C. Armstrong.

Inspector's Clerk: R. M. Rowley Morris.

Share Department: R. F. Peters, C. Halliwell.

Chief Accountant's Department: R. W. Gill *(Deputy Accountant)*, W. F. Smith *(Assistant Accountant)*, E. Dixon, T. C. Berry, F. O. Weylland, F. H. Sharp, C. R. Ashford, E. H. Gill, W. Lord, G. E. Steed, A. H. de Winton, H. L. R. Royse, E. H. Butcher, G. F. Mansell, G. Benzie, H. G. Treasure, C. E. Guest, F. R. Bennett, J. A. Sutherland, A. Perkins, J. F. Stewart, A. W. Brand, S. T. Smith, H. F. Scott, G. E. Fox Davies, F. W. Rogers, W. L. Crapp, F. T. Horniblow, H. S. Chapman, P. W. Rogers, C. E. Melville, F. A. Sutton, H. W. Stokes, T. Wallace, C. R. Senneck, H. P. Carter, C. W. Baily, L. A. Stanley, J. P. R. Scrivener, R. W. Manhire, F. King, H. H. Wicks, G. H. Fairbank, H. L. Stace, A. H. Wilson, A. J. Arnold, J. W. R. Nurse.

Stock and Coupon Department: F. Alexander *(Principal)*, R. Herbert *(Deputy)*, C. P. Santler, C. F. Gabb, E. W. Nuttall, F. W. Crimp, G. C. Woodward, C. B. Millard, C. H. Dearling, A. P. Carter, T. C. Merry.

Securities and Discount Department: F. Hawgood *(Principal)*, W. W. Wigg, W. T. Kelly, E. E. Knowles.

Foreign Department: W. M. Stevenson *(Pricnial)*, L. M. Potts, W. C. Haws, G. C. Holford, E. J. Everson, S. Dudley, C. G. Osborn, S. A. V. Hale, A. S. Busby, A. H. White, S. G. Manhire.

Country Clearing Department: W. Delleany *(Principal)*, E. J. Eastment, J. J. Sheldon, A. G. Blore, M. C. Acott, A. E. Voice, J. H. Brinson, A. A. Goodrich, R. M. Brailsford, J. O. Kirkley, H. L. Walker, M. G. Oakshett, J. W. Kemp, P. C. Ray, E. B. Owen, P. G. Betteridge, G. A. N. Cauldwell, C. Blumsum, L. W. Reynolds, C. W. P. Humphrey, S. G. Bunster, J. Mallet-Paret.

Town Clearing Department: A. Kemp *(Principal)*, H. Turner, F. Hall, E. P. Ray, J. G. Coxhead, J. Roberts, C. A. Bradley, S. Robson, G. W. Boyle, R. A. R. Mather.

Walks Department: J. Delleany *(Principal)*, E. A. Barnard, G. H. Stupart, C. B. Gray, H. Elkington, S. Wayling, A. S. Taylor, A. Bone, F. E. Powell, C. G. A. Brooks, J. Bromley, C. L. Penman, G. D. Gold, W. H. McLellan, L. da Costa, P. T. R. Gillett, G. H. Lewis, F. H. Haws, H. Turner, A. T. Gough, H. B. Geake, R. W. Bowly, B. G. Butler, G. R. Pimm, W. A. Smith.

Messengers: E. Brooks, H. Case, T. Saunders, J. Payne, B. Verrall, J. T. H. R. Cooper, J. Carvell, A. Henson, D. Spiller, H. J. Hill, T. Irving, G. Thorne, J. L. Aldhous, A. Carey, A. N. Catchpole, G. Birbeck, G. Seymour.

BIRMINGHAM HEAD OFFICE

Staff – Inspection Department: T. F. Shann, E. T. Boyce, F. A. Beane, J. H. Newton, F. G. Gibson, G. W. H. Biglen *(Chief Inspector's Confidential Clerk)*.

General Managers' Private Secretary: G. Ramsden.

Staff – Advance Department: J. H. Ford, A. R. Food, G. B. Grant, J. Griffiths, B. E. Reynolds, P. I. Lloyd, A. Bradley, J. A. Parish.

Secretary's Office: H. A. Haywood, W. H. Cooper, E. F. Horley, J. Peacock, T. H. Caswell, C. J. Freeman, P. E. Randel, G. S. C. Child, J. McMillan, R. H. Wilson, J. G. Blackhall.

Accountant's Department: D. Smart, A. B. B. Ragg, N. Stevens, W. H. Wright, J. H. Cooke, S. F. Firkin, C. M. Henderson, H. A. R. Butler, G. H. Sharpe, A. Hackney, H. C. Churley.

Bill Department: B. P. Miners, C. F. Gare, J. E. Cornforth, E. H. Smith.

Stationery Department: V. M. Bennett, *Superintendent*, A. B. Mathews.

Building Inspector: C. Gill.

Messengers: W. H. Young, F. J. Cooke, H. Watkins

LONDON

CITY OFFICE: 72 Lombard Street, EC – Harry B. Francis, *Manager*. A. Baird, A. J. W. Circuitt, *Assistant Managers*.

Staff: V. Alexander, E. W. Base, C. H. Passingham, W. C. Mould, G. W. J. Butcher, W. Tripp, G. W. Croxford, A. Stevenson, E. W. Scott, W. E. Smith, W. Turner, G. R. Sargent, J. W. Davis, C. W. Watts, A. B. Churchill, A. E. Pasbach, A. H. Browning, J. H. Philps, J. Charles, E. Kingsmill, B. Pringle, C. W. Nind, J. E. Collins, H. Chapman, F. Gray, F. C. Palmer, W. G. Earthy, R. H. Taylor, H. K. Money, E. J. Robson, A. C. Cooper, P. G. Martin, H. C. V. Davis, F. G. Hawkes, S. A. Matthews, A. W. Thorpe, F. E. Saxton, E. Westhorp, H. J. B. Pratt, W. G. Cauldwell, H. S. Carter, A. J. Hazleton, F. C. Trott, J. S. Mulbery, R. H. T. Abbs, A. S. L. Clarke, H. C. Fothergill, F. Bentley, H. R. Cope, E. C. Thomas, S. Williams, R. E. Holmes, E. G. Wilson, F. W. Morgan, W. E. Allnutt, A. J. Harris, C. H. Evans, C. Cockerill, J. G. Baker, P. C. Coltman, H. Stevenson, G. Pelham, W. A. Barnett, H. J. Caton, B. A. Hullett, C. Barritt, E. J. H. Holt, E. J. Thomas, L. J. Paige, H. J. Steddy, L. R. Zambra, H. H. Arnold, F. S. L. Kendall, J. N. Cundy, C. H. Lidwell, A. T. Hall, R. W. Ellis, E. R. Page, L. A. Matthews, C. M. Tuke, H. W. R. King, M. G. Morrison.

WEST END: 16 St James's Street, SW. – J. H. Ponsonby, *Manager.* R. Skipwith, *Assistant Manager.* Charles Hawkes, J. Thurston, *Sub-Managers.*

Staff: J. Baskett, R. E. Mills, W. Beal, H. Pound, E. Hughes, H. Nichols, W. Miller, J. Patterson, W. L. Kitson, B. P. Larkins, F. E. Langworth, E. A. F. Mould, G. J. Holt, A. R. L. Williams, A. F. G. Gape, H. Birch, A. H. Tilsley, H. E. Morgan, W. J. Lawson, S. F. Charlton, S. N. E. O'Halloran, A. F. V. Gibbon, H. H. Cowley, G. Whicher, F. Mason, F. J. Winterbottom, H. D. Ashford, M. Fraser, C. K. Gaylard, H. F. Tilsley, A. W. C. Hurrell, A. E. Leigh Bennett, H. S. Herbert, G. R. Godbold, E. S. Vickers, L. B. Johnson, J. M. Carter, Harold Thurston, B. W. H. Carter, H. L. Kitson, R. C. Baskett, J. D. Watts, F. N. Bartholomew, S. E. Mackay, Herbert Thurston, O. S. Leigh Bennett, L. H. de Fontaine, S. E. Hall, E. Kingston, C. G. M. Baye, C. F. Ponder, V. J. Smith, G. H. Savory, J. F. Pratt, W. L. Allden, R. W. Pattison, L. W. Wood, J. L. Leisk, H. L. Owens, H. O. James. *Messengers:* W. Ackland, H. Radmore, W. Bryant, W. A. Kennedy, G. Killick, F. Flebb.

LAW COURTS: 222 Strand, WC – Mackworth B. Praed, Herbert H. Twining, *Managers.* C. P. Johnston, *Assistant Manager.*

Staff: E. T. Clark, J. C. Tattersall, A. Yeates, J. H. Fuller, H. C. Sherring, S. Evison, L. W. Drake, A. Fletcher, A. H. B. Hughes, E. J. Marsh, W. J. Knowles, A. E. Salt, C. A. V. Becker, J. A. Barker, H. Gaster, A. E. Wright, H. S. Stallard, F. Hewetson, A. E. Bellringer, M. H. Williams, C. H. H. C. Harden, J. H. Downward, F. W. Elcome, R. F. A. Orr, W. S. F. Rowe, H. F. Jones, L. J. S. Hulse, W. G. Johns, H. Grant, G. S. Peck, H. C. Benger, H. L. Smith, H. W. Dorey, C. J. Salt, A. Martin, G. F. Palmer, J. C. Hunter, K. H. Coster, C. G. Thomas, G. B. Massingham, H. B. May, C. M. Brereton, H. D. G. Steer, A. R. Thompson, H. W. Salter, G. Paget, F. J. Bell, B. J. Crafer, W. J. Matcham, C. A. H. Hogg. *Messengers:* J. J. Wilson, G. T. Hooper, J. Johnson, J. H. Birt, J. Stephens, T. Thomas, B. J. Jackson, J. J. Binks.

CHEAPSIDE, EC – W. S. Draper, *Manager.*

Staff: H. E. Soward, T. H. Cooper, R. J. Martin, E. E. White, W. J. Rawlings, T. S. Allen, A. J. Percival, E. Carré, H. J. L. Ketchen, G. B. Jennings, R. M. J. Burke,

A. J. Cluer, T. L. H. Cheltnam, W. E. Simmons, J. A. Griffiths, O. W. Batt, W. G. Vandy, F. W. Foot, N. C. Day, F. M. Williams, A. F. Barrett, P. S. Streeter, P. J. A. Bolton, H. H. Barber, C. W. Hensman. *Messengers:* J. W. Candy, J. Bright, G. Chassereau, F. J. Wheeler, H. Wills.

ALDERSGATE STREET, EC – A. Wheeler, *Manager.*
Staff: E. Staines, F. H. Smith, E. Gramshaw.

BELGRAVE ROAD, SW – E. T. Janson, *Manager.*
Staff: S. F. Denny, E. W. Hughes, G. W. Webster, E. F. Smith, F. H. Little, B. E. Dickins, J. F. Smith, R. Wylie. *Messenger:* H. J. Catchpole.

EAST CITY (Fenchurch Street) – C. F. Smythe, *Manager.*
Staff: J. McKnight, W. J. Loder, C. E. Streatfield, P. R. H. Earthy, J. H. Cole.

FINCHLEY ROAD, NW – H. Holyoake, *Manager.*
Staff: C. Seabrook, S. P. Mole, G. A. McKenny.

HAMPSTEAD (Rosslyn Hill, NW) – S. R. Scott, *Manager.*
Staff: R. H. Penson, C. H. Lindop, S. Hilhouse, H. A. N. North, C. S. Levy, F. S. Orme, N. C. Reid.

HOLBORN CIRCUS, EC – S. J. Martin, *Manager.*
Staff: S. W. H. Huntly, E. C. Barnard, C. T. McDowall, M. B. Hoare, E. H. Dixon, A. C. W. Horne, B. W. Haws, J. M. Bray. *Messenger:* S. Marshall.

PADDINGTON (Cambridge Street, W) – W. L. Harris, *Manager.*
Staff: F. P. Cope, T. C. George.

WEST KENSINGTON (Hammersmith Road, W) – A. A. Bell, *Manager.*
Staff: H. T. Belcher, A. Hills, C. S. Hoare, C. G. Hallpike, R. W. Heenan, W. H. James.

BIRMINGHAM AND DISTRICT

COLMORE ROW – W. H. South, *Manager.* G. Baxter, S. Price, *Sub-Managers.*

Staff: A. Brindley, A. Jagger, A. W. Maxon, D. R. Griffiths, J. Beck, W. C. Fletcher, E. J. Miners, W. J. Nelson, P. H. Goode, A. P. Pike, C. W. Pearson, B. A. Yates, R. L. Meats, H. S. J. Nicol, J. J. K. Smith, J. U. Wright, H. A. Blewitt, T. H. Harris, A. W. Smith, A. H. Haynes, J. H. Richardson, T. Derry, F. W. Blackburn, P. L. Jewsbury, H. W. Forster, H. Hadley, F. C. Jarvis, F. A. Wharton, F. B. Watton, A. R. Williams, A. P. Gold, T. Williams, G. W. Elderkin, W. H. Nichols, C. W. Hadley, J. W. Loach, H. A. Ragg, J. G. Cooksey, S. T. Keys, W. Robinson, S. Ford. *Messengers:* A. Young, J. Harding.

HIGH STREET – James Randall, *Manager.*
Staff: W. E. Anderson, J. Partridge, G. F. Smith, W. C. Key, W. T. A. Perry, C. Harper, T. H. Harrison, F. W. Reeve, H. L. Mortimore, F. W. Wright, J. R. Smallwood, E. Price, W. H. Avery, W. E. Pickering, M. Edwards, E. A. Raybould, F. B. Price, W. F. Gould, J. C. Green, W. H. Summerton, A. G. Wedgwood, J. J. Bibby, G. Gregg, E. A. Horrocks, G. E. H. Round, R. W. Mellor, J. B. A. Hatfield, H. M. Purser, C. J. Corbett, J. F. Hobbes, J. G. Walker. *Messenger:* C. F. Edwards.

TEMPLE ROW – F. H. Jordan, *Manager*. F. Young, *Sub-Manager*.

Staff: J. Toleman, D. A. Hartley, C. H. Phillips, G. W. Wynn, R. Churley, T. V. Newill, J. E. Hempseed, S. H. Stilton, J. A. Wood, J. S. Yeoman, F. J. Hands, E. L. Holt, W. Lambie, W. H. Key, C. W. H. Curtis, G. H. Block, T. Elderkin, H. B. Hartill, W. H. C. Briant, H. Harvey, C. T. Matthews, H. J. Robathan, E. A. Rogers, E. J. Marshall, D. H. A. Smith. *Messengers:* W. H. Stanton, F. Clayton.

NEW STREET – J. Y. Anderson, *Manager*.

Staff: W. Sutherland, W. G. Luckman, W. D. Roach, H. Greey, A. W. Freeman, F. Jolly, A. E. Caldicott, G. F. Tranter, H. Fewings, J. F. Bain, A. G. Hall, G. H. Brothwood, J. F. N. Bach. *Messenger:* F. Bracey.

ASTON ROAD – E. Shaw, *Manager*.

Staff: H. J. Vernon, J. H. Walter, C. F. Hewitson, F. A. Woodcock, C. J. Tovey.

BLOOMSBURY (Great Lister Street) – Eric A. Goode, *Manager*.

Staff: P. V. Cuthbe, J. Sutherland.

BRISTOL STREET – J. R. Houghton, *Manager*.

Staff: H. A. Hallam, W. E. Dimelow, A. E. Dain, N. C. Pollock, J. A. Hidson.

DERITEND – John Phillips, *Manager*.

Staff: W. J. Woodward, C. S. H. Clarke, W. Filkin, A. J. Nixon, G. W. Evans, F. Satchwell, F. Shaw.

DUDLEY ROAD – Charles Miller, *Manager*.

Staff: W. H. Fowler, H. W. Chamberlain, H. S. Newton.

EDGBASTON (Five Ways) – F. H. Steeds, *Manager*.

Staff: J. H. Goode, W. N. Harrison, F. J. Greening, G. C. Watson, C. Brindley, F. E. Burkitt, T. Edmonds, F. Ramsden.

GOOCH STREET – W. B. Stokes, *Manager*.

Staff: V. Vaughan, C. E. Adams, A. H. Brindley, S. Rogers, L. Pettitt.

GREAT HAMPTON STREET – C. J. L. Hickling, *Manager*.

Staff: R. E. Old, W. C. Key, A. J. Wheat, S. P. H. Cantrill, W. J. Derry, H. Caink, E. J. Hardy, J. L. Noake, H. Hanford. *Messenger:* A. G. Clayton.

HANDSWORTH (Villa Road) – E. T. Awdry, *Manager*.

Staff: W. B. Swannock, M. East, F. H. Pritchard, A. W. Samuel.

HARBORNE – H. Maxon, *Manager*.

Clerk: E. Bloomer.

HIGHGATE (Moseley Road, Camp Hill) – W. D. Hindmarsh, *Manager*.

Staff: C. R. P. Barton, A. W. Davis.

JAMAICA ROW – Charles Bailey, *Manager*.

Staff: A. J. Woodward, H. M. Finnis.

LADYWOOD (Monument Road) – Offley Wade, *Manager*.

Staff: W. R. Little, O. A. Garner.

MOSELEY (Alcester Road) – Albert Smith, *Manager*.

Staff: H. J. E. Turner, J. M. Sutherland, P. G. Wright, T. E. Phillips.

PARADE – E. T. Rudge, *Manager*.

Staff: J. C. Bourne, F. E. Kempson.

SELLY OAK – B. L. Burges, *Manager*.

Staff: R. Baugh, E. A. Evans.

SMALL HEATH (Coventry Road) – John Phillips, *Manager*.

Staff: W. T. Jones *(Clerk in Charge)*, H. C. Jones, N. A. Haywood.

SPARKBROOK (Stratford Road) – J. Ryan Bell, *Manager*.

Staff: J. Tovey, E. J. Birkett, C. H. Marston, L. O. Butler, G. B. Hutchings.

STIRCHLEY AND BOURNVILLE – B. L. Burges, *Manager*.

Staff: W. H. Osborn, J. B. Adams.

Sub-Branch: King's Norton, *Staff:* E. G. Howard *(Clerk in Charge)*, W. J. Hackney.

COUNTRY

ABERDARE – W. F. P. de Winton, *Manager*.

Staff: W. Edwards, J. E. Lewis, M. C. Davis, O. Williams, W. W. Bunning, G. H. Mountjoy, W. H. Hall, J. H. O. Harpur, J. P. Davies.

ABERGAVENNY – C. E. Davies, *Manager*.

Staff: H. G. Stanway, G. H. Evans.

ALNWICK – A. W. Simpson, *Manager*.

Staff: C. Davidson, E. Tate.

ALTRINCHAM – R. R. Kirby, *Manager*.

Staff: H. A. Pearce, W. Greenleaves, C. Power, W. Taylor, J. Dewar. *Messenger:* H. R. Meredith.

AMLWCH – Samuel H. Smith, *Manager*.

Staff: R. W. A. Davies, C. G. Williams.

ANNFIELD PLAIN – W. C. Hann, *Manager*.

Clerk: Thomas Kay,

ASHBOURN – Edward Hunter, *Manager*.

Staff: H. F. Gibson, R. V. Beare, W. W. Goodhead, W. S. Rose.

ASHBY-DE-LA-ZOUCH – *Staff:* A. B. Morris *(Clerk in Charge)*. C. Ivins.

ASHFORD – W. F. B. Jemmett, *Manager*.

Staff: F. W. Amos, A. R. Knight, A. J. Davis, J. Sykes, H. H. Andrews, E. Dyson, S. E. Amos, H. P. Thornhill. *Messenger:* J. Dyson.

ASHINGTON – A. F. D. Bell, *Manager*.

Clerk: J. Blair.

ATHERSTONE – William Marshall, *Manager*.

Staff: H. T. Elkington, E. T. Bell.

AYLESBURY – F. W. Attwood, *Manager.*
Staff: J. C. W. Ellis, E. N. N. Bartlett, E. E. Wright, E. H. Bawcutt, J. A. Castle.

BANBURY – T. I. Webb-Bowen, *Manager.*
Staff: W. G. Page, H. Swain, W. H. Butler, T. Smith, W. G. Hill.

BANGOR – James Smith, *Manager.*
Staff: W. Morgan, H. J. Evans, R. W. Pritchard, H. M. Baker, R. W. Roberts, H. G. Williams, C. Jones.

BARRY DOCKS – R. C. Cullum, *Manager.*
Staff: P. Mavins, J. W. G. Morgan.

BATH – Leonard C. Hare, *Manager.*
Staff: A. Trenfield, R. O'Dowd, H. J. Knapp, C. L. Perry.

BEAUMARIS – James Smith, *Manager.*
Staff: D. C. Davis, E. R. Oliver.

BELLINGHAM (Northumberland) – Edward Dixon, *Manager.*
Clerk: J. H. Iveson.

BEXHILL-ON-SEA – C. Drayton Greenwood, *Manager.*
Staff: V. H. Müller, R. A. Bourdeaux, F. Cluer.

BIRKENHEAD, WEST END (Shrewsbury Road) – J. W. Woodley, *Manager.*
Clerk: H. E. Bushell.

BIRKENHEAD (Borough Road) – J. W. Woodley, *Manager.*
Staff: E. Quaile, jun., G. Duguid.

BIRKENHEAD (Charing Cross) – J. W. Woodley, *Manager.*
Staff: H. T. M. Jeffrey, J. E. Thomas.

BIRTLEY (Co Durham) – J. H. Rippon, *Manager.*
Clerk: J. Sinclair.

BLACKBURN – C. W. Eastwood, J. B. Close, *Managers.*
Staff: I. S. Martin, J. Livesey, D. J. Haworth, C. W. Shepherd, C. E. Slatter, H. Foster, W. Pickup, R. V. Walsh, P. B. Broadbent, W. B. Foulds, W. C. Baxter, T. Gibson. *Messengers:* T. Parrott, F. H. Coombs.

BLACKHILL (Co Durham) – R. G. Barclay, *Manager.*
Clerk: William Russell.

BLAYDON-ON-TYNE – C. Robson, *Manager.*
Clerk: M. H. Lee.

BLOXWICH – Walter Blackburn, *Manager.*
Staff: G. C. Townshend *(Clerk in Charge),* J. S. Price.

BLYTH (Northumberland) – John Kirsopp, *Manager.*
Clerk: G. G. Smith.

BOURNEMOUTH – Walter T. Gale, *Manager.*
Staff: R. C. Wilton, E. T. S. Ottley. *Messenger:* C. Clark.

BRACKLEY – W. G. Hemmings, *Manager.*
Clerk: R. W. Farmborough.

BRACKNELL – C. Phillips, *Manager.*
Clerk: E. Milton.

BRECON – James Morgan, *Manager.*
Staff: C. H. de Winton, A. A. Davies, H. W. Evans, W. J. Thomas, H. D. Owen.

BRIDGEND – Wm Watkins, *Manager.*
Staff: T. M. Cule, J. M. Griffith, S. Lewis.

BRIDGNORTH – Thomas Powell, *Manager.*
Staff: F. S. Wilson, T. W. Sheppard, A. R. Denton, F. G. Miller, N. L. Smith.

BRIGHTON – Samuel Twining, *Manager.*
Staff: J. H. C. Johnston, G. Baker, R. F. Round. *Messenger:* J. A. Killick.

BRISTOL (Corn Street) – W. O. Coward, *Manager.* G. A. Ireson, *Assistant Manager.*
Staff: A. Leonard, C. A. E. Abbott, A. T. Curtler, W. H. Jane, J. C. Kynoch, L. C. Lawrence, H. J. Hare, E. J. Tapson, J. H. Simpkins, J. F. Squire, G. R. A. Hardiman, R. Richards, W. E. F. Peake, D. J. Tate, C. A. Roberts, A. V. N. Russell, M. D. Lucas, A. V. C. Dunsford, C. J. Fussell, R. M. T. Lisle. *Messenger:* J. Morley.

BRISTOL (Bedminster) – W. O. Coward, *Manager.*
Staff: A. Lee *(Clerk in Charge),* P. Meggs.

BRISTOL (St Philip's) – E. Flight, *Manager.*
Staff: G. R. Adams, J. Knight, F. L. Much, G. S. Roberts, C. H. W. Challenger.

BRISTOL (Stokes Croft) – J. H. Reynalds, *Manager.*
Staff: H. F. Banner, J. B. Lea, L. W. Marshall, R. H. Gainer, A. S. D. Pearce.

BRISTOL (Temple Gate) – J. Mortimer, *Manager.*
Staff: E. W. Thuell, T. C. Wade, E. N. Puddy.
Sub-Branch: Totterdown, *Clerk:* H. L. Butt.

BROADSTAIRS – W. B. Urry, *Manager.*
Staff: C. A. Hayward, H. A. Poulton, P. P. Johnson.

BROMSGROVE – L. Gibson, *Manager.*
Staff: P. C. Newill, G. L. More, F. G. Maylett, F. Hughes.

BROSELEY – J. A. Downes, *Manager.*
Staff: H. R. Botwood, G. B. Ledger, M. A. Powell.

BUCKINGHAM – H. Freegard, *Manager.*
Staff: A. J. Kay, A. N. D. Lang, F. Lydiatt, W. Cooper.

BURFORD (Oxon) – A. J. Herbert, *Manager.*
Clerk: C. B. Foster.

BURSLEM – C. W. Davies, *Manager.*
Staff: F. Marks, P. Hitchings.

BURTON-ON-TRENT (High Street) – E. A. Brown, *District Manager.* C. R. Harrison, *Sub-Manager.*
Staff: R. R. Morley, R. Peach, W. Allen, O. J. Greensmith, W. Lobb, C. Shaw, J. A. Jones, J. Husband, J. F. Giles, C. W. Gammidge, F. W. Spencer, R. D. Briggs, E. B. Stokes, T. J. Lusty, E. R. Squire, P. S. Neale, S. F. Smith, W. H. C. Cooke, A. R. West, E. R. Hunter, F. E. White, J. S. Piddocke, W. L. Thomas, H. W. Faulkner.

BURTON-ON-TRENT (Borough Road) – C. T. Clarke, *Manager.*
Staff: F. R. Hobbes, S. R. West, F. T. Dallison, D. S. Hawley.

CANNOCK – C. F. Greatorex, *Manager.*
Staff: G. T. Green, R. H. L. Dodgson, J. A. Swindell.

CANTERBURY – T. B. Blain, *Manager.*
Staff: P. G. T. Logan, C. W. Stevens.

CARDIFF – W. S. de Winton, *District Manager.* C. Hensman, *Manager.*
Staff: H. J. Davis, T. S. Davies, D. Till, R. T. Richards, T. Williams, E. C. Lovett, T. O. Williams, R. M. Evans, C. Collier, A. L. J. Newton, J. P. Griffiths, N. G. Piddocke, G. O. Morgan, W. S. Stephens, R. H. Green, C. M. Hensman, W. L. G. Williams, G. A. Kynch, J. M. Griffith, J. H. Morgan, J. Lowdon, H. E. C. Björkmann, D. E. Owen, J. C. P. Crosby, W. P. Davies, A. J. Conroy. *Messengers:* S. Hollis, C. King.
Sub-Branches: Penarth – *Staff:* G. D. Westland *(Clerk in Charge)*, P. I. Scott, W. N. Harris.
Canton – *Staff:* J. D. Blackie *(Clerk in Charge)*, J. L. du Sautoy.
Roath – *Staff:* F. Burrell *(Clerk in Charge)*, G. S. Haines.

CARDIFF DOCKS – A. Brown, *Manager.*
Staff: E. B. Thomas, R. S. Edmonds, F. C. Parker, J. S. Jones, S. I. Collier, R. J. Tanner, E. W. Evans, R. Owen, T. L. Mortimer, S. J. Davies, W. R. Bown. *Messenger:* J. Flint.

CARDIGAN – W. Lewis, *Manager.*
Staff: W. R. Richards, E. O. Evans, J. Jones, J. J. Jones, J. Phillips.
Sun-Branches: *Agent* – Thomas Jenkins.

CARMARTHEN – Albert Harries, *Manager.*
Staff: J. D. Jones, E. M. Yorath, J. P. Lewis, J. Lewis.

CARNARVON – G. H. Humphreys, *Manager.*
Staff: P. W. Griffith, G. F. Jackson, E. J. Pughe, H. L. Jones, A. L. Roberts, R. E. Hughes, J. P. Griffiths.

CATERHAM VALLEY – R. P. Nyren, *Manager.*
Staff: A. E. Morgan, J. B. Theweneti, L. Fraser, R. T. Batchelar.

CHATHAM – P. L. W. Coltman, *Manager.*
Staff: H. R. Swatman, O. L. Triphook.

CHELTENHAM – F. F. Leaver, *Manager.*
Staff: F. E. Ward, C. M. Kirk, M. V. K. A. Bowie, C. Downes, J. E. Manners, M. G. Heelas, W. M. Bain, H. W. Broom, S. H. Lawrence, A. G. Taynton, C. A. Smith, H. R. Jennings, E. S. C. White, C. C. Chamberlain, C. F. R. Barnett, A. H. G. Harries, F. Lusty, W. Smith, A. R. N. Joseland, A. Turner, B. Wiseman, R. W. Callender, A. G. Madgwick, O. H. Chester, D. Thomas, E. L. Brown, H. A. Henson. *Messenger:* E. Mortimer.
Sub-Branches: Montpellier – *Staff:* C. W. C. Baxter *(Clerk in Charge)*, H. E. Daniel.
Winchcomb: *Agent:* A. L. Hall.

CHESHAM – E. W. Clarke, *Manager.*
Staff: E. G. Fossick, A. E. Bateman.

CHESTER – Francis Skipwith, *Manager.* J. Dodds, *Sub-Manager.*
Staff: T. S. Bowles, A. G. Ayrton, B. F. Oxenbould, T. B. Barnett, A. R. Trafford, E. A. Thwaites, W. L. Cameron-Davies, W. H. Elley, H. Partington, J. A. Vincent, W. W. Waldron, W. R. H. Hallmark, W. A. Jones, W. H. Evans, E. Stockton, R. H. Griffith, T. A. Siddall, W. P. Gamon. *Messenger:* W. Rathbone.

CHESTER-LE-STREET (Co Durham) – F. C. Bullock, *Manager.*
Clerk: F. J. Ryle.

CINDERFORD – S. W. Hadingham, *Manager.*
Staff: S. P. Barker, W. F. Coomber.

CIRENCESTER – W. Wearing, *Manager.*
Staff: T. Avenell, W. E. Attwood, A. Bryant, T. A. Arden, D. R. Hellings, E. G. Hall.
Sub-Branch: Cricklade – *Agent:* J. H. Franklin.

CLIFTON (Bristol) – H. C. Rowe, *Manager.*
Staff: H. W. Hobkirk, H. T. Webb, L. Frampton.

COALVILLE – W. C. Tomlinson, *Manager.*
Staff: W. G. Allen, W. Wright.

COLESHILL – T. B. Woodward, *Manager.*
Clerk: H. B. Dudley.

CONSETT – Robert E. Kirsopp, *Manager.*
Staff: W. R. Raistrick, S. H. Eltringham.

COVENTRY – F. H. Ragg, *Manager.* J. Mountfort, *Sub-Manager*
Staff: A. Heginbottom, J. S. Weatherilt, H. Mountfort, C. E. Rotherham, F. H. B. Smith, W. J. Healey, A. F. Day, H. J. Bennett, V. W. B. Wearing, E. M. Davies, J. W. Blower, C. G. Irving, B. W. Pattman. *Messenger:* J. Lee.
Sub-Branch: Foleshill – *Staff:* J. B. Morris *(Clerk in Charge)*, R. O. Orton.

DARLASTON – W. H. Briant, *Manager.*
Staff: D. Steel, F. H. Purser, C. K. Deakin.

DARTMOUTH – W. R. Elliott, *Manager.*
Clerk: L. G. M. Horder.

DARWEN – P. C. Winterton, *Manager.*
Clerk: R. S. Ashton. *Messenger:* G. Edge.

DEAL – C. A. Wylde, *Manager.*
Staff: G. W. Hoare, L. A. Lewis, P. G. Wood.

DERBY – A. White, *Manager.*
Staff: A. H. Harris, C. Barrington.

DOUGLAS (Isle of Man) – G. R. Bargery, *Manager.*
Staff: W. Dean, T. G. Aylen, J. R. Moore, H. H. Cowin.

DOVER – J. R. Munday, *Manager.*
Staff: C. Muriel, O. W. F. Thomas, W. N. Britton.

DOWLAIS – T. R. Nicholas, *Manager.*
Staff: A. E. Davies, E. Williams.

DROITWICH – J. Harrison, *Manager.*
Staff: W. C. Blakeway, A. C. Pickering jnr., R. D. Salter.

DUDLEY – J. Nichols, *Manager.*
Staff: W. H. Smith, E. L. Bindschadler, F. Corbett, C. R. Wordsworth, R. C. Hall, R. D. Stockton, J. E. Shann, W. L. Freer. *Messenger:* W. Maycock.

DURHAM – W. C. Fulthorpe, *Manager.*
Staff: H. Johnson, C. B. Veitch, R. Salkeld.

DURSLEY – F. Davis, *Manager.*
Staff: H. C. Allen, G. J. Grafton.

EAST GRINSTEAD – H. W. Harding, *Manager.*
Staff: C. F. Bowen, C. H. Mead, C. H. Whidborne, M. G. Smith.

EASTBOURNE – T. Ryde Jones, *Manager.*
Staff: C. W. F. Harris, E. P. Richardson.

EDENBRIDGE – C. H. James, *Manager.*
Clerk: L. L. Saunders.

ELLESMERE – F. J. Lindop, *Manager.*
Clerk: E. E. Wilshaw.

ENFIELD – H. Balfour, *Manager.*
Staff: W. G. Waters, F. D. Short, G. W. L. Croxford, P. F. Sparling.

ERDINGTON – A. Harris, *Manager.*
Staff: W. G. Miller *(Clerk in Charge),* J. E. R. Guyton, C. Berry.

EVESHAM – P. Choules, *Manager.*
Staff: A. M. Lloyd, G. W. Beale, S. A. Gothard, R. E. Twigg, R. B. Walton.
Sub-Branch: Bidford *Agent:* E. J. Sill.

FARINGDON – W. W. Bliss, *Manager.*
Staff: P. T. Owen, G. A. C. Williams, J. K. Eaton, P. S. Emerton.

FENTON (Staffs) – A. L. Smith, *Manager.*
Staff: F. H. Pilsbury, A. Coates.

FISHPONDS (Bristol) – F. G. Tucker, *Manager.*
Staff: C. V. Hancock, E. W. Stenner, G. M. Hall.

FOLKESTONE – J. R. Martin, *Manager.*
Staff: H. F. P. Carpenter, P. S. Reeves, E. H. Rudkin, A. G. Clarke, C. R. Wind.

GATESHEAD – J. J. Gibson, *Manager.*
Staff: W. A. Mowitt, S. Wilson, F. Ferry, W. Sordy.

GLOUCESTER – J. A. Smithin, *Manager.*
Staff: A. E. Pullin, A. L. Brown, H. P. Haine, W. D. Stone, L. H. Carter, E. R. Parker, W. J. Manning, A. C. Smith, C. L. Saunders, A. E. Pardington. *Messenger:* H. Baxter.

GREAT BRIDGE – G. T. Gibson, *Manager.*
Staff: C. E. Vernon, R. E. Piercy, A. H. Tennison.

HALESOWEN – F. D. Nutt, *Manager.*
Staff: W. H. Woodward, S. H. Abraham, W. J. Garratt.

HANLEY – F. S. Stringer, *Manager.*
Staff: G. Brindley, E. E. A. Stilton, J. Lamont, B. A. Smith, E. H. Playfer, E. W. Smith, R. W. Leadley. *Messenger:* John Baskerville.

HASTINGS – H. C. Willmott, *Manager.*
Staff: G. McCormick, W. T. Love, E. J. McCormick, W. J. Parker, A. A. Bull, F. Skinner, G. S. Cavey, W. H. Matthews, F. J. Mann, E. A. Malpas, F. H. Owen, H. Cox, V. L. Courcier, A. J. Eden, J. C. Daly, M. L. Roscher. *Messenger:* A. H. Pickford.

HAVERFORDWEST – Arthur Say, *Manager.*
Staff: S. H. K. Wilson, H. J. Charles, F. T. Brown, J. L. Lloyds, D. Jones, S. M. Jones.
Sub-Branches: Fishguard *Agent:* G. A. Roberts.
Milford Haven – T. Y. Lewis *(Clerk in Charge),* P. Jones.
St David's – *Agent:* J. M. Williams.

HAWARDEN – James Frater, *Manager.*
Staff: F. W. Pughe, H. Moore, W. M. Evans, M. Roberts, J. Provis.

HEMEL HEMPSTEAD – W. Summerfield, *Manager.*
Staff: C. F. Page, E. Elliott, W. W. Engall, J. W. Creaghe, R. J. H. Hunt.

HEREFORD – T. Williams Allen, *Manager.*
Staff: C. H. Woodhouse, H. E. Whatley, V. H. Pembridge, T. R. Day, B. W. Hussey-Freke, E. S. de Woolfson.

HESWALL (Cheshire) – H. Newsom, *Manager.*
Clerk: E. A. Dickins.

HEXHAM – William Crichton, *Manager.*
Staff: B. A. Iveson, E. Davidson, F. E. Umpleby.

HORLEY – W. Dawson, *Manager.*
Staff: A. H. White, E. H. Belcher.

HOVE (Brighton) – S. Twining, *Manager.*
Staff: J. W. Talbot *(Clerk in Charge),* B. C. Whitfield, C. K. A. Congreve.

IRON BRIDGE – J. W. White, *Manager.*
Staff: H. B. Coney, W. Andrews, C. B. Ledger, W. E. Osborne.

JARROW – William McDowell, *Manager.*
Staff: H. Borgeest, J. P. Dancaster.

KIDDERMINSTER – H. M. Newcomb, *Manager.*
Staff: J. F. Coney, H. L. Powell, W. F. Woodward, G. L. Potter, H. E. Hughes, F. E. Knapp, W. P. Day. *Messenger:* H. Fildes.

KINGSBRIDGE – W. S. Seaton, *Manager.*
Staff: J. J. Mansfield, E. J. S. Molyneux.

KINGSWOOD (Bristol) – A. B. Philip, *Manager.*
Staff: E. L. Miller, V. Mitchell, J. O. Clay.

LEAMINGTON – A. C. Pickering, *Manager.*
Staff: W. Bach, R. B. Braithwaite, H. E. Hake, A. T. Bowen, W. B. Hunt, P. F. Keys-Wells, C. M. Tomson, R. J. Nason, A. C. Hoare, W. J. Robinson, F. H. Ragg, jun., A. C. Nuttall, K. V. Cowie, W. C. Masters, W. J. Dashwood. *Messenger:* J. Stapleton.

Sub-Branches: Kenilworth – *Staff:* G. A. Bishop *(Clerk in Charge),* W. C. Buckland.
Southam – E. F. Squires *(Clerk in Charge).*

LEEDS – R. Wilson, J. W. Fowler, *Managers.*
Staff: J. Arnott, S. J. W. Hannam, J. Coates, S. Crabtree, F. Pilley, H. Porteous, W. H. Thompson, A. Townsley, J. E. Myers, J. Kilburn, C. V. Myers, A. E. Batman, J. F. Balfour, S. J. Cole, J. W. I'anson, F. E. Jennings, T. Cracknell, W. S. North, R. A. Wilson, L. S. Dobson, R. M. Bilton, W. H. Reed, G. S. Douthwaite, N. K. Jones, A. R. Oates, C. A. Allen, F. W. Chester, B. H. Edrupt, A. Tillotson, A. S. Harrison, G. C. Edrupt. *Messengers:* P. Ling, J. H. Ricketts.

LEEDS (Hunslet) – H. W. Peck, *Manager.*
Staff: G. Harrison, E. Giles.

LEICESTER – T. Burdett, *Manager.*
Staff: A. Lole, A. Wright, W. C. Horne, S. A. Pywell, C. R. W. Cuckson, F. Hopps, A. C. Cooper, A. W. B. Overton, J. Bradley Smith, R. Severn Smith, R. G. Rae, J. N. Boughton, J. A. Jones, L. R. Hyde, W. A. Davis, T. Andrews. *Messenger:* J. Gillings.

LEOMINSTER – J. A. Daggs, *Manager.*
Staff: H. A. Cross, E. R. Williams, B. Shinner, A. L. M. Stephens.
Sub-Branch: Weobley – *Agent:* F. H. Leather.

LICHFIELD – W. B. Wordsworth, *Manager.*
Staff: J. F. Dixon, F. Wright, R. M. Meacham, N. Harris, G. R. Couch.

LIVERPOOL (Brunswick Street) – J. McKay, *District Manager.* J. Smitton, *Manager.*
Staff: W. H. Priestley, T. Newsom, G. C. Newstead, R. Bell, J. Watson, C. H. Macdona, J. Montgomery, jun., E. F. Agnew, R. Andrew, C. M. Hamilton, G. S. Carroll, W. J. Sutton, J. M. Davidson, H. A. Jeffs, P. McLay, H. W. B. Stanswood, S. A. Williams, C. M. Haley, W. H. Barrow Williams, T. Priestley, S. J. Simpson, C. E. Grisewood, W. L. Ker, L. W. Drinkwater, A. W. Sedgwick, A. W. Healey, R. L. Crosbie, R. Fairclough, E. Hannay, P. R. Sutton, A. G. Henderson, P. G. Haswell, J. W. Hay, E. F. Bushby, G. C. Scarlin, O. Walford, A. Quaile, E. P. Crowther, jun., J. N. Veitch, B. Oxton, S. P. Hill, J. Harper, S. N. Thomas, A. Fleming, W. T. Ellis, H. le P. Newstead, H. E. Maw, L. G. Mackenzie, R. A. Hitch, P. W. Hawkes. *Messengers:* A. Childs, J. Davies.

LIVERPOOL (Exchange) – Thomas Holder, *Manager.*
Staff: H. Clibborn, F. S. Glass, C. C. W. Ray, G. A. Lawson, F. C. S. Anderson, W. G. Bovill, D. Charles, R. H. Kelly, A. Brettargh, R. O. Johnson, A. H. Jones. *Messenger:* T. Bridge.

LIVERPOOL (Bold Street) – J. Isaacson, *Manager.*
Staff: J. Richardson, E. M. Jackson, A. G. Ashcroft, R. L. B. Buckler, W. A. S. Owens, G. C. Leece.

LIVERPOOL (London Road) – T. A. Baron, *Manager.*
Staff: A. H. Barnett, C. F. Price, H. Halsall.

LIVERPOOL (Parks Branch, Lodge Lane) – J. FF. MaGrath, *Manager.*
Staff: H. N. Meek, S. P. Bevis.

LIVERPOOL (Princes Road Branch, Upper Stanhope Street) – G. D. Noon, *Manager.*
Clerk: C. Ross.

LIVERPOOL (Sefton Park and Mossley Hill) – Herbert Lawson, *Manager.*
Clerk: P. D. D. Barker.

LLANDUDNO – J. H. Rees, *Manager.*
Clerk: F. D. Jones.

LLANDYSSUL – A. Harries, *Manager.*
Staff: W. G. Edwards *(Clerk in Charge),* D. J. H. Evans.

LLANELLY – A. Evans, *Manager.*
Staff: H. M. Griffiths, A. S. Jones, W. Jennings, H. E. George, S. I. Rake.

LLANFAIRFECHAN – James Smith, *Manager.*
Staff: G. H. Nicholls *(Clerk in Charge),* A. M. Jones.

LONGTON – G. F. Ann, *Manager.*
Staff: C. T. Forrester, E. D. Lloyd, E. Mackrory, W. J. Tomlinson, E. C. Trew, E. Fletcher, A. R. Jones, G. F. Stringer. *Messenger:* J. C. Wood.

LOUGHBOROUGH – C. L. Ferneley, *Manager.*
Staff: A. R. Thomas, E. J. Tucker.

LUDLOW – E. L. Mylius, *Manager.*
Staff: J. E. G. Bowen, G. K. Graham, F. F. Prosser, W. P. Rees.

MAIDENHEAD – H. J. Mount, *Manager.*
Staff: F. C. Webster, A. T. Taylor, C. Headington, H. D. Loosley, M. H. Cleaver, L. E. Samman.

MAIDSTONE – W. Holyoake, *Manager.*
Staff: H. L. Young, F. E. H. Lang, H. L. Urry, T. W. J. N. Thomas, L. G. Bailey.

MALVERN – C. B. Stokes, *Manager.*
Staff: L. G. Birkmyre, E. S. Bentley, F. W. King, J. O. Leigh-Lye, C. M. Evans, C. H. Humphreys.
Sub-Branch: Malvern Link – *Agent:* C. Woodhouse.

MANCHESTER – R. M. Platt, H. F. B. Moore, *Managers.*
Staff: G. Suttle, A. B. Harvey, R. T. Miller, E. W. Barton, W. Ogden, A. P. Holt, A. Buckley, F. J. Deakin, H. A. Bowman, T. T. Fawcett, C. J. Slade, G. Barker, W. Power, L. Letherbrow, W. E. Hughes, J. H. Longshaw, J. W. Rickards, P. Suttle, S. T. Hunter, J. C. Pickin, A. Prinsep, E. J. Elvy, G. F. Upcher, H. W. Milne, J. H. Sproston, S. Parkes, J. A. Kellet, R. E. Eckersley, A. Worthington, H. W. Moss, A. Clayton, A. N. Long, G. F. Buckland, P. H. Paulsen, A. S. Burd, S. E. Warren, W. H. Rains, H. C. Heathcote, A. Jones, W. B. Brown, E. C. Purdy. *Messengers:* A. Longbottom, C. Cox, A. Crossland, W. G. Edwards.

MARGATE – A. B. Cobb, *Manager.*
Staff: S. S. McDowall, H. Linnell, H. A. Vasse, F. M. Dunstan, S. de C. Child, S. J. Lowe, A. Smith, D. L. Downes, J. R. Mackie. *Messenger:* D. Hitchcock.

MARGATE (Cliftonville) – W. H. Linnell, *Manager.*
Staff: E. W. F. Barton, J. Wood.

MARLOW – George Loosley, *Manager.*
Staff: J. S. Manlove, R. A. W. Collett.

MELTON MOWBRAY – T. Burdett, *Manager.*
Staff: A. E. Pywell (*Clerk in Charge*), J. Lambrick.

MERTHYR TYDFIL – W. J. Mountjoy, *Manager.*
Staff: J. C. Williams, H. Isaac, F. G. Bowen, W. E. Thomas, J. J. Thomas, J. A. Thomas.

MONMOUTH – C. H. Payne, *Manager.*
Staff: W. J. Richards, J. Lane, A. Phillips.

MORLEY – W. McKnight, *Manager.*
Staff: H. Schofield, F. J. F. Waddington.

MORPETH – Ralph Crawford, *Manager.*
Staff: C. E. Proctor, J. S. Matthews, R. G. Dand.

NETHERTON (Staffs) – J. Nichols, *Manager.*
Staff: W. A. Shaw (*Clerk in Charge*), T. F. Homer.

NEW SWINDON – Lyttelton Etty, *Manager.*
Staff: W. M. Masters (*Clerk in Charge*), A. E. Appleby, G. F. T. Banks, C. L. Hill.

NEWBIGGIN-BY-THE-SEA – A. F. D. Bell, *Manager.*
Clerk: J. Blair.

NEWCASTLE-UPON-TYNE – John Smith, *Manager.*
Staff: J. S. Bertram, J. Cocks, W. J. Watson, J. B. Wilson, W. M. Simpson, W. G. Ferry, G. W. Burtt, J. G. A. Borgeest, C. Shelmerdine, J. Reay, J. W. Dick, E. S. Farish, R. J. Greenwell, T. Garnett, J. K. Wardhaugh, J. R. Hood, C. Alderson, J. T. L. Pattinson, J. Williamson, A. Sutherland, G. Hardie, R. R. T. Shepherd, T. Gibb, G. P. Stephenson, E. E. Johnson, R. Hudson, C. D. Bell, W. O. Atkinson, J. Ainsley, J. Lyon, J. E. Armstrong, C. T. Brown, A. E. Gray, R. Story, A. Dobson, J. T. Porteous, E. Church, T. W. Lee, J. Saul, T. Middlemiss, B. Tansley. *Messengers:* R. Watson, J. Sander.

NEWCASTLE-UPON-TYNE (Byker Branch, Shields Road) – A. W. Burn, *Manager.*
Staff: J. W. Watson, G. W. Lambton.

NEWCASTLE-UPON-TYNE (Gosforth Branch) – W. H. Sowerby, *Manager.*

NEWCASTLE-UPON-TYNE (Osborne Road Branch) – W. Blakey, *Manager.*
Clerk: H. H. Thwaites.

NEWCASTLE-UPON-TYNE (Scotswood Road Branch) – Percy B. Balfour, *Manager.*
Clerk: M. T. Hindson.

NEWCASTLE-UPON-TYNE (Westgate Road Branch) – C. J. Sambidge, *Manager.*
Staff: F. L. Robinson, T. Nicholson, E. C. Good.

NEWCASTLE (Staffs) – H. Everill, *Manager.*
Staff: G. J. Green, C. W. Salt, A. J. W. Dicks, A. J. Richards.

NEWNHAM (Glos) – S. W. Hadingham, *Manager.*
Staff: E. S. Boissier, H. K. Ault.

NEWPORT (Mon) – Leonard Acomb, *Manager.*
Staff: W. H. Miller, S. Ferrabec, A. G. Sargent, W. Clark, F. Williams, W. H. Kersey, T. C. Morgan, L. G. Graham, J. C. Jenkins, B. H. Lewis, B. Mountjoy, A. F. Stratton, W. J. Davies. *Messenger:* W. R. Hewitt.
Sub-Branch: Abertillery – *Staff:* B. Lewis (*Clerk in Charge*), D. Jones.

NEWPORT (Salop) – E. M. Webster, *Manager.*
Staff: A. Milner, C. W. S. Dixon, F. H. Morris, E. P. Kelly.

NORTH SHIELDS – J. S. Spence, *Manager.*
Staff: F. P. Moore, J. M. Lishman, F. P. Moore, jun., W. C. Thwaites, J. Porter, F. J. Spence.

NORTHAMPTON – H. E. Roberts, *Manager.*
Staff: G. Reynolds, A. C. Fowke, E. G. Fellows.

NOTTINGHAM – Henry Russell, *Manager.*
Staff: W. E. Hemming, G. G. Gadd, W. Merchant, E. H. Wilson, W. E. Holbrook, W. Richards, F. Mountjoy, C. O. Jones, F. R. Hole, C. Simpson, G. B. Hall, O. E. Walker, W. R. D. Twyning, R. D. North, E. Fell, A. M. Ellis. *Messenger:* E. J. Butcher.

NOTTINGHAM (Alfreton Road) – J. Budd, *Manager.*
Staff: C. W. Hall, F. O. Stote, S. J. T. Eacott, A. E. Griffith.

NUNEATON – A. V. Curtler, *Manager.*
Staff: F. E. Buswell, W.M. Cranstoun.

OLDBURY – E. H. Wedgwood, *Manager.*
Staff: G. Osborn, G. H. Melley, H. W. Rushton, J. F. Yeatman, L. G. Biglen, S. E. Burn.

OSWESTRY – G. S. Tovey, *Manager.*
Staff: C. E. W. Noake, F. J. H. Grant, S. H. Griffiths.

OXFORD – H. W. Hudson, *Manager.*
Staff: S. M. Goodman, G. M. Thomas.

OXTED – Stanley Lawrence, *Manager.*
Staff: G. H. Cosens, H. G. St Q. Isaacson.

PAIGNTON – Thomas Arnold, *Manager.*
Staff: D. W. Howat, A. W. G. Mercer.

PEEL (Isle of Man) – G. R. Bargery, *Manager.*
Staff: T. C. Good, H. J. Killip.

PERSHORE – W. T. Pace, *Manager.*
Clerk: O. D. Hamer.

PONTYPOOL – H. H. Pratt, *Manager.*
Staff: J. M. James, J. R. Jones, W. H. Thomas, H. J. Hughes.

PONTYPRIDD – R. A. Lewis, *Manager.*
Staff: A. B. Black, T. J. Evans, E. R. Thomas, J. T. Edwards, T. P. Davies, J. S. Hughes, H. Crump, S. G. Harris, W. D. Thomas, T. G. Davies, J. B. Evans.

PORT TALBOT – R. R. Chalk, *Manager.*
Staff: W. H. Gabriel, F. H. Tristram.

PRESTEIGNE – J. S. Day, *Manager.*
Staff: J. Mackintosh, G. B. James.

RAMSEY (Isle of Man) – G. R. Bargery, *Manager.*
Staff: T. E. Acheson *(Clerk in Charge),* E. G. Teare.

RAMSGATE – A. C. Downes, *Manager.*
Staff: J. Coleman, A. C. Urry.

READING – R. Penson, *Manager.*
Staff: J. R. Cook, B. Ruddock, W. R. Cusden, F. W. Hart, W. J. Lowe, O. E. White, T. W. Lawrence, A. C. G. Tregay, J. Avent, C. J. Crew, P. C. Wright. *Messenger:* C. Cook.
Sub-Branch: Oxford Road, Reading – R. W. Cusden *(Clerk in Charge).*

REDDITCH – G. Galbraith, *Manager.*
Staff: S. S. Stone, E. F. Talbot.
Sub-Branches: Alvechurch – *Agent:* J. W. Partridge.
Astwood Bank – *Agent:* E. Perkins.

ROSS – F. P. Fitch, *Manager.*
Staff: W. H. B. Cowx, C. J. Knight.

ROTHBURY – J. P. Ridley, *Manager.*
Staff: N. Snaith, J. Brodie.

RUGBY – A. Russell Cox, *Manager.*
Staff: S. Parkinson, W. D. Muriel, A. G. Youngman, H. T. Webb, J. G. Tudor, H. C. Franklin, A. R. R. Green.

RUGELEY – A. H. Pratt, *Manager.*
Staff: G. L. Teare, C. R. Underhill.
Sub-Branch: Hednesford – *Staff:* W. H. Frith *(Clerk in Charge),* H. W. M. Handford.

RYE – C. H. Stenning, *Manager.*
Staff: A. Stocks, H. R. Russell, C. G. Davis.

ST GEORGES (Bristol) – A. B. Philp, *Manager.*
Staff: R. A. Pickin *(Clerk in Charge),* A. Carter.

ST LEONARDS-ON-SEA – H. C. Willmott, *Manager.*
Staff: A. H. Lucy *(Clerk in Charge),* E. D. Collins, F. Barden, H. Ransom, H. Lloyd, C. S. Monckton. *Messenger:* W. J. Miller.

SALE – W. H. Dixon, *Manager.*
Staff: W. Bott, A. Matheson.

SALTAIRE – James Brooks, *Manager.*
Staff: T. W. E. Carver, T. Pickles.

SANDGATE AND SHORNCLIFFE – R. J. Fynmore, *Manager.*
Staff: T. C. Kirk, P. Jackling, A. L. Stokes.

SEVENOAKS – R. P. Evans, *Manager.*
Staff: H. J. Hensman, W. P. Ingall.

SHIFNAL – G. H. Gaydon, *Manager.*
Staff: G. H. Nock, W. W. Owen, W. I. Galbraith.

SHIPSTON-ON-STOUR – S. F. Ellis, *Manager.*
Staff: W. Johnson, G. G. Bloomer.

SHOTLEY BRIDGE – R. G. Barclay, *Manager.*
Staff: G. H. Walton, W. W. Hamilton.

SHREWSBURY – N. E. Tidy, *Manager.*
Staff: E. W. Belcher, R. Mytton, G. Hobbs, G. H. D. Coates, A. E. Lloyd, J. W. Phillips, G. F. Seers, J. E. Davies, W. R. Miller.

SMETHWICK – J. A. Goode, *Manager.*
Staff: J. W. Braithwaite, H. S. Fellows, D. M. Holland, C. Pain.
SOLIHULL – J. Marshall, *Manager.*
Staff: O. W. Bridgwood, H. Towler.

SOUTHBOROUGH – F. W. Tracy, *Manager.*
Staff: J. R. Thomas, C. A. Thompson.

SOUTH SHIELDS – C. Rewcastle, *Manager.*
Staff: G. Hannay, W. M. Hudson, J. Robson, W. Lambton, A. Lawson, W. D. Wait, P. Cooper, J. L. Coll, G. C. Waugh, A. E. Willins, E. A. Mearns. *Messenger:* A. Duncan.

STAFFORD – P. H. Harston, *Manager.*
Staff: J. C. Smith, J. Walker, G. Wain, W. T. Shaw, R. H. Webb, J. A. Robinson, F. Gobey, H. H. N. Edwards, H. J. J. Pritchard, C. J. Tomlinson, M. H. M. M. White, H. Marshall, G. R. Davies. *Messenger:* A. Mackenzie.

STANLEY (Co Durham) – H. Y. Ridley, *Manager.*
Clerk: W. T. Dixon.

STAPLE HILL (near Bristol) – F. G. Tucker, *Manager.*
Staff: W. H. Pickin, J. Edwards.

STONY STRATFORD – G. W. Bull, *Manager.*
Staff: A. F. Fraser, H. Freegard, jun., G. E. de M. Lewin, G. V. Stilliard.

STRATFORD-ON-AVON – S. F. Ellis, *Manager.*
Staff: H. T. Hickling, A. Chattaway, T. E. Hill, H. E. Britton, F. R. Bore.

STROUD – A. Dunsford, *Manager.*
Staff: G. S. J. Cubitt, T. F. Bastin, J. W. Buye, W. T. Lorimer, H. R. Peake, H. Chambers, F. E. Tyler, E. V. Gardner, C. R. M. Gale. *Messenger:* W. J. Goscomb.

SUNDERLAND – J. J. Garnett, *Manager.*
Staff: J. H. Forsyth, J. P. Walker.

SUTTON COLDFIELD – A. Harris, *Manager.*
Staff: C. H. C. Clifford, L. B. Griffin, F. C. Baxter, R. Gabb, V. H. S. Betton.

SWADLINCOTE – E. K. L. Lawson, *Manager.*
Staff: J. A. Murray, A. H. H. Rugg, R. H. Wheddon.

SWANSEA – E. P. Bowen, *Manager.*
Staff: T. T. Walters, A. E. Finch, A. W. Heywood, T. M. Bellingham, H. L. Morgan, E. A. Chalk, R. E. Wall. *Messenger:* D. Webb.

SWINDON – Lyttelton Etty, *Manager.*
Staff: R. M. Bentley Taylor, C. H. Fletcher, W. J. L. Read, H. C. Vicker, R. E. J. Sparks, W. R. Desages.

TAMWORTH – W. B. Fowler, *Manager.*
Staff: G. P. Fulcher, L. J. Owen, R. Clarke.

TENBURY – J. C. Tearne, *Manager.*
Staff: W. J. Shinner, G. R. Baxter, F. S. Roper.

TENTERDEN – C. H. Stenning, *Manager.*
Staff: J. W. Eden *(Clerk in Charge),* F. W. Borman.

TETBURY – A. Appleby, *Manager.*
Staff: H. B. Perrins, C. H. Todd.

THAME – J. E. D. Ostrehan, *Manager.*
Staff: T. W. Robinson, S. Shaw, D. J. Dixie, A. G. Lloyd.

TONBRIDGE – S. W. Burgess, *Manager.*
Staff: G. E. Skinner, P. E. Collins, F. B. Carlisle, H. D. Brown, P. W. Anderson.

TORQUAY – Lewis W. G. Butler, *Manager.*
Staff: T. Marshall, R. J. Clode, A. H. Fitzgerald, S. P. Hutchings, E. Candish, F. G. S. Taylor, G. M. Newton, C. J. Molineaux, E. W. Clancey, E. J. F. Lyon, F. A. Sully, B. H. E. Richardson, G. S. Seaton, H. B. Thomson.

TORRE – Lewis W. G. Butler, *Manager.*
Staff: R. Glasby *(Clerk in Charge),* G. A. Tully.

TUNBRIDGE WELLS – H. A. Beeching, *Manager.*
Staff: H. P. C. Hare, W. H. Ashby, E. S. Kerbey, M. K. Whitaker, G. Cherry, W. U. Boreham, H. O. Cowley, A. Keeley, D. S. Hole, C. E. Longley, B. M. Rumbold, H. S. Dennington, G. A. King, A. H. Owen, W. R. Courtenay, J. G. R. Harris. *Messenger:* J. W. Pickford.
Sub-Branch: Pantiles, Tunbridge Wells – H. R. Walker *(Clerk in Charge).*

UTTOXETER – S. R. Fletcher, *Manager.*
Staff: T. B. Speechly, A. H. Brown, W. H. Durrad, A. Hunter.

WALLSEND – A. Constable, *Manager.*
Staff: C. M. Johnson, J. Liddell, R. T. Lloyd.

WALSALL – W. Blackburn, *Manager,* W. G. Pratt, *Sub-Manager.*
Staff: H. N. Blackburn, D. T. L. Hadley, J. Jackson, F. J. L. Neads, C. P. Askin, A. T. Humphries, C. H. Sampson, S. G. Hawksford, J. A. J. Briant, W. M. Buck, A. E. Arnold. *Messenger:* E. W. Burnham.

WARWICK – S. C. Smith, *Manager.*
Staff: C. G. Irving, A. R. Bain, S. P. Cherrington, C. H. Niven, N. B. St John Cowie, A. J. Price, A. J. Campbell.
Sub-Branch: Kineton – *Agent:* J. Griffin.

WATFORD – W. H. Cookes, *Manager.*
Staff: J. T. Gardner, C. J. Hudson, H. Ager, H. R. Riley, A. Oakman, W. H. Overton, E. A. Clarke.

WEALDSTONE – W. H. Cookes, *Manager.*
Staff: Edward Hudson *(Clerk in Charge),* W. M. Eldridge.

WEDNESBURY – J. H. Prince, *Manager.*
Staff: A. Jackson, H. Thompson, H. Nivison, F. W. Gaydon, E. J. Kirby.

WELLINGTON (Salop) – J. Galbraith, *Manager.*
Staff: A. H. Smith, J. S. Barker, W. H. Nicholls, A. O. Joynson, F. E. G. Botwood, T. F. Lowe.

WELSHPOOL – M. Powell, *Manager.*
Staff: H. W. Evett, H. Blackith, H. W. Simmons, W. Owen.

WEST BROMWICH – H. M. Gunning, *Manager.*
Staff: G. R. Downward, W. H. W. Coachafer, A. S. Goodman, A. H. Jackson.

WESTGATE-ON-SEA – G. H. Hitchin, *Manager.*
Staff: A. W. Saunders, F. V. Barrow, A. L. Downes.

WHITCHURCH (Salop) – W. J. Corbishley, *Manager.*
Staff: J. Baugh, E. W. Wilkinson.

WILLENHALL – W. H. Briant, *Manager.*
Staff: T. Wilkes, C. R. Lyons, T. P. Beeston.

WINSLOW – E. R. Mayor, *Manager.*
Staff: W. E. Law, W. S. Watkins.

WOLVERHAMPTON – J. S. Dixon, *Manager.*
Staff: A. T. South, S. E. Smith, W. D. Durant, A. J. Tucker, C. H. Cotterill, J. H. Nurse, J. J. Dobbs, J. Ewart, H. Lee, R. E. Plant, G. H. Barcroft, G. A. Birch, A. Warlow, A. D. Young, W. T. Grainger. *Messenger:* W. Oakley.

WORCESTER – H. E. Tovey, *Manager.*
Staff: G. F. Abell, C. Hunt, P. Lane, H. J. Guest, J. T. W. Read, W. Page, H. Powell, J. S. Gouldbourn, D. H. K. Sayer, S. P. Maylett, J. Gabb, H. R. Kissack, W. Hobbs, R. A. N. Hall, T. S. Owen, E. N. W. Johnston. *Messenger:* E. Ballard.

WORTHING – F. B. Tilt, *Manager.*
Staff: A. W. Harpur, W. C. Brereton.

WOTTON-UNDER-EDGE – W. Heath, *Manager.*
Staff: J. Reade, S. W. Russell.

WREXHAM – G. Frater, *Manager.*
Staff: W. R. Wilson, A. E. Whitfield, C. T. Owen, H. M. Bull.

Retirement in 2006

Just like Mr Lloyd featured on page 121 retirees in 2006 also received an invitation from the Bank. The luncheon has now expanded into a three day seminar which includes two dinners, two luncheons and two full English breakfasts. Rosemary Rippon reports:

'Retirees together with their spouse or partner are invited away for three days. In some cases this involves a drive down to *Cricklade Hotel and Country Club*, set in over 30 acres of peaceful, secluded grounds on the edge of the Cotswolds and boasts a leisure centre with Romanesque swimming pool and a nine hole golf course. Different venues are held throughout the country.

The seminar starts with tea and cakes on arrival at 5pm. My seminar which was run on 19-21 April 2006 for 33 delegates was chaired by a retired training manager from Private Banking, Tony Kite, who told us he had run the marathon and loved walking. Of the retirees seven were taking voluntary early retirement whilst the remaining ten were approaching the retirement age of 55 for a woman and 60 for a man.

The seminar started with an introduction by Tony who told us that gone were the days when you worked for 50 years and, lived if you were lucky for another five. Retirement was no longer regarded as "God's Waiting Room" and new opportunities abounded. We learned that the aim of every retiree should be to draw a pension for longer than he/she had been paid a salary. In order to obtain this, healthy living and exercise were recommended. We were informed that walking was a good form of exercise. All staff grades from Grade 1 down to Grade 8 came through the seminars. Retirement was a great leveller!

We listed all the problems associated with retirement namely health, money, relationships, fear of the unknown and time management. We were urged to pursue additional interests such as joining U3A (University of the Third Age) a learning cooperative of older people which enables members to share, educational, creative, and leisure activities. He urged us not to rush into things like he had done. He explained that a neighbour had suggested that as he now had nothing to do he might like to take on the task of driving a stroke victim to rehabilitation once a week. Tony agreed and for the next three years found himself driving that stroke victim to tend the garden at the centre. When he was approached to act as trustee of the charity he agreed on condition that someone else was found to take over the role as driver.

During the course of the seminar we learned that the key to a successful retirement was to be positive, rise early, be organised, make lists and keep a calendar, be flexible and change your mind if it does not suit you. The wheel of retirement comprised of the following segments: education, social, entertaining, holidays and sports.

During the Retirement Planning Seminar the topics covered were: The Challenge of Retirement, Making the Most of Retirement, State Benefits, Long Term Care, Crime Reduction, Financial Planning, Health in Retirement and an optional Job Search.

The session on General Health by Dr Ken Wray, a very fit 86-year-old retired General Practitioner proved to be most entertaining and informative. He told us to watch our weight, drink five or six glasses of water a day, and watch our intake of alcohol. Cereals like porridge provided the body with roughage. It was very important to get your blood pressure checked every two years with the ideal reading being 130/80. Regular visits to the optician were recommended as 95% of glaucoma was found this way. A urine test for sugar was recommended every two years. It was stressed that exercise preserved the heart muscle and mind.

He told us the story of a colleague who worked in the Accident and Emergency department of the local hospital. One day a young singer with pierced rings who sang in a local pop group was bought in with abdominal pains. The doctor examined her and was surprised to notice that her pubic hair was dyed green with a tattoo above which stated "Keep off the Grass". The doctor had to operate for appendicitis and left the following note on the patient "So sorry, I had to mow the lawn".

The seminar provided us with the opportunity of talking to colleagues and their spouses and sharing our different experiences. We all left with a feeling of wellbeing and comradeship. Driving home we reflected on our well organised and informative "retirement break" and felt that Lloyds TSB had done us proud.'

The following is an extract from a speech made by Roger Lord following his retirement. His initial interview for a job in 1962 took place at Lloyds Bank Ltd, Head Office, 71 Lombard Street, London. Everyone who wanted to join the Bank had to go to that office for an interview. Another applicant that day was from South Shields. Travel expenses were reimbursed.

'I joined the staff on the 3 September 1962 at Colchester branch – well someone had to join the staff there. Now how can I describe Colchester branch? This was a branch where rigid formalities served, where you wore a suit, shirt and tie. One hot summer's day just after 3pm when the bank had shut I loosened my tie and was severely reprimanded by the First Board Manager for daring to do such a thing.

This was a branch where the staff mostly consisted of men who had fought in the Second World War and most of them were still busy fighting it. The First Cashier used to click his heels, military style. "You can't do that in the army and you can't do it here" he used to say. Then there was the Head of Securities section. Electricity had yet to reach the lift so the trolleys were pushed onto it and wound up by means of a large wheel. You then applied the brake when it reached the top. I used to have to wind up the securities trolley. The Head of Securities could not wind the trolley on account of his war disability for which he received a pension. It maybe lacked that hint of glamour to hurt his back lifting something onto a lorry in Darlington.

A new lift was installed at Colchester branch. It stuck near the floor where I was machine room supervisor. I heard the alarm and thought it was out in the street. From the inside of the lift Mr Taylor started shouting my name. "Go and tell Mr Jenkins" (office manager). It probably did not help when I said "Right, stay where you are". Taylor and Jenkins did not get on, so this was a moment to savour. When I got down there, I paused beside his open office. "Yes, what do you want?" asked Mr Jenkins, I replied: "Mr Taylor is stuck in the lift". A line of sniggers went along the row of cashiers. Mr Jenkins did not immediately reply. He sat with his head in his hands, shaking with the effort of not bursting out laughing. Finally, he recovered his composure and said "All right, Lordy, I'll deal with it" Lordy? That amounted to a term of endearment! I was usually just plain Lord.

When I started my first job all I did was bang rubber stamps onto cheques and do machine lists (list cheques and agree totals). After a year I was sent off down to the sub-branch which was not in a very glamorous part of town. It was the kind of branch where local prostitutes used to pay in Monday morning. The cashier used to say "My word Rosie you have had a good weekend."

I was under Bob, a big chap, for training. He was the son of a police sergeant. He was an amiable man, the kind of man you would trust with your life savings. He got four years for fraud. There was something he was not telling me! Years later I saw him driving through the streets of Slough in a much more expensive car than I was driving. I made enquiries and was told after he got out of prison he worked in security- a security company that is.

My next move was to Sydney Street Cambridge. This was a big office with 100 people on the ground floor. They put me onto the counter next to a man called Sid. Now the drawers of Sid's till were stuffed with pornographic books and bananas. One day Sid opened his drawer and as a mark of great favour to me offered me a banana. I was then sent to work with the Head Cashier, Mr Dawes. I don't think he had a first name and if you did know it you dare not use it, as he was such a formidable man.

Now the office manager was a man called Reggie. One lunch hour, when Reggie was not there, Sid the banana man went to Reggie's desk to look for something. He pulled the draw out and there in front of him was a handgun. Sid in a panic went off to get Mr Dawes, who then lined everyone up and gave a practical demonstration on how you unloaded that particular model.

One Saturday morning I worked with Cyril who was acting as the Head Cashier. At 11 am he said go and hide in the basement and just keep out of Pat Dillon's way. Pat was the Office Manager's Assistant and he was in charge that morning. When I went down into the basement I have never seen so many people before. It was crowded down there! I eventually emerged at 11.29 and 30 seconds and met Pat Dillon (the bank shut at 11.30am to the public and the staff went home at 12 noon). Have you finished on that till? Oh go and help add up the cashier's sheets.

After Cambridge I was sent to Chorleywood. I did not even know where it was. There were three staff namely the manager, me and a girl. The manager was Mr Tidy - like something Queen Victoria left behind. He had a starched white collar and felt that people who worked in the Bank should have private means. He told me that during the War he had served in Africa – Johannesburg that is. It did cross my mind that Johannesburg was not exactly in the front line. I decided to say nothing as he had to write my report on which my salary depended.

At the end of 1967 I went to Aylesbury branch. Some 15 months later I was transferred to Princes Risborough – another time warp! The two men running the place were still living in the wartime paper shortage. The manager used to open the post in the morning and slit the envelopes and lay them flat. When a customer came in and they needed to write out an authority he wrote them on the back of an envelope. Yes, Mr Richardson had an acute worry about paper. In 1971 with decimalisation one of my jobs was to take away all the £ s d vouchers and throw them away. However Mr Richardson found them and bought them back out again and said they could be used as scrap paper. Yes you know what happened, the cashiers used the £ s d vouchers instead of the new decimal ones. I had to stick them in my pockets and secrete them out of the office.

I then went to Slough where I was not particularly happy. Whilst at this branch I had a row with the personnel manager – well what else are they for. They were barriers to progress – you wanted to progress and they wanted to hold you down on the grounds they wanted you to fill the jobs. During a blazing row one day he said "You are an able man, would you like to go on an Outward Bound course? I said "Yes". That was the end of that conversation. A few months later I was sent for by one of the managers. He said with a leering smile on his face: "Do you know where Moray is?" Getting out a map he pointed to Scotland and the NE corner, "You are going there." I said "I like it." He said "In January."

The pre-course notes were not encouraging: "Sponsors should ensure that candidates have clothing suitable for a severe climate." The day I got there we were split into groups of between 12 and 13 people. Three of the group were teenagers. I belonged to one of the more mature groups, after all I was 27. I was thinking they will leave all the rough stuff for the boys – they won't bother with us. My illusions were shattered when a tall lean hard looking man with the kind of face that smiling was a total stranger to walked in. He said: "Right lads my name is Giles that is spelt B A S T A R D." He was the hardest instructor of the lot.

The next day we went out and found ourselves looking at a 10 foot high wall. What is that for, we thought? We soon found out. We were told that the record for 13 men going over this wall was 58 seconds. Giles said "Get over it …. Get over it I said." One man went over "Right lads you've had 60 seconds and you have only got one man over. You are going to have to do better with this." Actually we did, at the end of the course in the inter-team contest we got all 13 men over in 1 minute and 12 seconds.'

After Slough branch Roger served at Winslow, Great Missenden and finally Aylesbury Securities Centre where he saw the staff increase from 15 to 45. He retired on Friday 2 January 2004 having completed 41 years' service.

Branches

In 2008 a British film featured the 1971 raid on Baker Street branch. It became known as 'The Walkie Talkie' robbery and was one of Britain's most infamous crimes. A radio ham eavesdropped on a walkie talkie conversation between members of the gang whist they were at work breaking into the branch. One of the comments was: "We're sitting on £300,000". Mr Rowlands, the radio ham, recorded the messages and called the police. Detector vans were sent out and toured the area within a ten mile radius but they were unable to locate the bank robbers who were digging a 30ft tunnel from a rented shop into the bank vault. This 1971 picture shows customers making enquiries following the discovery of the bank raid.

Miss Lloyds Bank, Jackie Pool and the legendary black horse open the 390th office of Black Horse Agencies Stimpsons, Aylesbury, 1987. In 1991 the star of the bank's TV ads, Kustos, a ten-year-old was considered too old to continue and was replaced by younger horses, Beato and Cancara. In 1994 Cancara was voted the most popular horse by a well- known riding magazine. With his owner he supports charitable events all over the country.

Aylesbury's It's a Knockout, July 1990. Aylesbury branch won the competition. Simon Pinnel dumps colleague Georgina Clements in the tank. The winning team consisted of Simon Pinnell and his wife Sharon, Margaret Stacey, Paul McFarlane, Louise Harrison and Jason Evans.

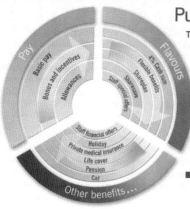

Putting it all together

This wheel shows many of the elements in your total reward package. Depending on your band, you could also be eligible for a company car (or cash allowance) and free private medical insurance. You may also be eligible for life cover, and for membership of a company pension scheme.

Don't forget the other elements of your employment package. In addition to those shown in the wheel, you also have access to:

- life event leave
- learning and development opportunities through the University for Lloyds TSB
- flexible working through Work Options
- parental leave
- a range of health and well-being benefits, guidance and support – including Healthcare Direct
- sports & social membership (including special events and offers)
- Matched Giving Scheme
- Give-As-You-Earn charitable giving scheme
- preferential deals on new and used cars through Cars4staff.

Junior Bank Clerks were nearly always required in Luton. This advert appeared in the Luton News in 1996. The benefits package in 'Putting it all together' appeared in a staff magazine in c2000.

In 1950 the Bank bought The Beacon, *a hotel in Hindhead, Surrey, to use as a training centre. In July 2000, eight of the original trainers and some of their spouses returned to Hindhead for a reunion. From left to right: Roland Smith (principal), Mrs Glen Ellis, Mrs Beryl McKie, Miss Jocelyn Edmonds (secretary), Roy Ellis (instructor), Alan Wilkinson (instructor), Mrs Helen Smith née Green (receptionist later moving on to management), Miss Poppy Sharpe (instructor), Mrs Brenda Scammell (instructor), Mrs Joan Wilkinson (delegate at the Training Centre), and Sandie McKie (instructor).*

Pictured is the new regional headquarters for Lloyds Bank on the Triangle Business Park at Stoke Mandeville, 1991. A site in Thame was looked at but it was decided that this two-storey building would be ideal. The building was purpose built for the Bank at a cost of 3½ million by Pearce Construction of Weybridge on behalf of site developers, Aylesbury-based Crosstyle. The van parked outside used to call every day to sell sandwiches and rolls to the staff. In 1992 the building won an award for energy conservation. John Bentley-Leek, Deputy Regional Architect for Lloyds said: 'In these offices we have been able to provide first class standards of comfort with a 20 per cent reduction in energy consumption. The sign on the wall reads: 'Regional Executive Office, Thames Valley and Eastern, Black Horse Financial Services.'

Staff at Aylesbury International branch are pictured in fancy dress costume raising funds for Red Nose Day, 1993.

Customer, England cricket captain Alastair Cook, visits the Leighton Buzzard branch of the Halifax which is part of the Lloyds Banking Group. Banking consultant, Deanna Plummer, welcomes the famous cricketer in 2015.

Aylesbury International Branch, c1993. Pictured above are Nikki Smith and Chris Barney. A lovely open plan office with plenty of carpark spaces and views over a green field. Despite the advent of computers the abundance of paper can be seen everywhere.

Strand branch (Wellington Street, Aldwych) in 1939 after a gelignite bomb was thrown at the building. In all, five bombs were thrown at targets in the West End of London and 19 people were injured. The bombs were thrown by terrorists of the Irish Republican Army. Police can be seen on guard near the wrecked windows of the branch, 25 June 1939. Today this Edwardian building, now protected by English Heritage, has been turned into a hotel and restaurant. The hotel is known as One Aldwych *and the restaurant and bar is called* Axis.

The nude charity calendar began as a fundraiser conceived by the ladies of the Rylestone and District Women's Institute and inspired a myriad of other groups to follow suit. Staff at Hertford branch decided to issue their own calendar to raise funds for the local Isabel Hospice, 2004.

"*The Manager at Lloyds Bank will know*"

For the average man, the occasion to make an important financial decision may seldom arise. But when it does, the man with an account at Lloyds Bank knows he can turn unhesitatingly to his branch manager for any information he may need to give him a clear, objective picture of the situation on which he must make a decision.

Let **LLOYDS BANK**

look after *your* interests

Golfing themed advert, 'The manager at Lloyds Bank will know' c1949. Compare this with the modern notices below stating 'Our Values' to staff as they take one of the glass lifts in the entrance hall at the head office in Gresham Street. The three values are: Putting Customers First, Keeping it Simple and Making a Difference Together.

Thanks for the Memory

'**Entered bank** in 1923 at a salary of £52pa with an extra £10pa for working in Birmingham. A 50 hour week...60 hour week for three weeks at each half yearly balance time, June and December!'
Pensioner Mr E. Jackson-Stevens of Glastonbury, *BIFU Report* 1990.

R.K. Powell remembers the instructions he received from Head Office Staff Department. 'I started on 1 March 1926 at Mountain Ash branch. I was told to wear a black coat and waistcoat, grey striped trousers, white shirt with stiff linen collar, dark tie, bowler hat and rolled umbrella. This was not a big city branch but a small branch in South Wales with a staff of seven or eight (all men).'

Roger Gilbert writing in 1993:
'This week I joined the ranks of the pensioners after working for Lloyds Bank for the best part of 30 years. I was a senior manager in the commercial banking division but the recession had brought about major changes to the job which at times could be very unsatisfying.

Jobs are fast disappearing across the financial services sector and Lloyds is no exception. So when the opportunity came to retire early, I volunteered. The bank has a very generous voluntary early retirement scheme, which means I shall end up with a pension of around £24,000 a year as well as a substantial tax-free lump sum.'

Wells branch was refurbished in 1990 which prompted a letter from a pensioner, Mr T.F. Harding to the assistant manager Roger Griffin. Extracts were provided to Lloyds Bank News in 1991:
'I started in the Bank at Wells in 1924. Mr Witt, the Cashier, smoked an incredibly foul pipe and the Second Cashier, Mr Reynolds, used to bring his sheepdog into the office every day. It spent its time under the Cash Book desk, and on wet days contributed to the general atmosphere!

During the early part of my time at Wells, the telephone was installed. It was in the Manager's room (Mr F. O. Stote) and I think he was the only one who knew how to use it!

The junior had to stoke the fire at the back of the office, and it was difficult to keep it right to please everyone.

Looking back, life was pretty good in those days, even though my salary was £8 13s 4d a month and my 'digs' cost £1 5s per week.'

Mr G. M. Warry, pensioner, wrote in 1989:
'Studying for the Institute of Bankers exams was an essential part of one's professional training, going back to World War 1. During my time those aspiring to management were expected to pass both parts and thus become Cert AIB.'

The importance of the Institute exams was mentioned in the Staff Induction Book, c1988:
Any member of staff who is interested may study for a series of examinations to become an Associate of the Chartered Institute of Bankers. This qualification is a must for those who'd like to get into management, although it's no guarantee of success.

The booklet went on to clarify Training for Management:
'If your work within the branch shows particular promise you may be selected for accelerated training through the Management Development Programme. To be selected you must earn a recommendation by your manager to go before a regional panel of assessors. Selection will mean your progress will be regularly reviewed although you will be expected to do well in your Banking examinations. In the long term, it should certainly enhance your prospects of making it into management.'

In 1962 it was decided to computerise Pall Mall branch. Machine operator at the time, Jeanette Hadley wrote in 1989 to Advance.
'Looking back the original idea was to computerise the Mechanisation Department of Pall Mall, then the potential for the rest of the bank was realised. Many branch managers were not always in agreement; we were sheltered but they had to face irate customers. There were many trials and tribulations. Air conditioning breaking down in the summer;

change of year; Leap year; missed deadlines - to mention just a few.

Geoff Bush, an IBM engineer was magic. He literally Posted accounts by reading the lights and placing the RAMAC arm onto the correct account. During a Charges run he kept us going by holding a machine together with string when no spare part was available.

The bank became the showplace with many foreign visitors coming to learn from our experience. We never had time to get bored because the Bank kept advancing, buying new generations of equipment, adding more routines of banking and having to expand premises.

I joined the bank in October 1951 and took early retirement in May 1986 at Third Board level. I am grateful to the bank for giving me the opportunity which has resulted in my living in Tenerife - what I call my "Fantasy Island".

The things I miss most now that I am in retirement is the sense of humour which kept us going at times, also the comradeship and the sense of achievement and pride especially when things went well.'

In 1991 *Lloyds Bank News* wrote:

'A customer called to open a current account; his application was scored by machine- and refused. Then the letter advising him of this decision was returned marked "not known at this address". Branch manager John Dobson reckons this proves that the machine does make some good decisions.'

A male bank clerk going on a Junior Course at Hindhead in 1962 could expect to be given a badge –green if over 18 and red if under 18. Two bars served drinks. One was for the over 18-year-olds and the other was for those under the age of 18. The alternative was a nearby pub that did not ask many questions.

The women machine operatives used to teach the boys the rudiments of the machine room. There were no girls on the course. It was not uncommon to receive a letter stating that you were being transferred to another branch of the bank. You were ordered to report immediately the course was finished to your new branch without going back to your old branch.

Sir Brian Pitman, who died aged 78, after suffering a heart attack, was widely regarded as the most successful banker of his generation. In the 18 years up to 2001, as chief executive and then chairman of Lloyds Bank, he transformed it from the smallest of the original Big Four high street banks to one of the largest and certainly the most successful in financial terms. Pitman worked for the bank virtually all his adult life having joined his local Cheltenham branch as a 21-year-old in 1952.

In 2010 *Financial World* learning of the demise of Sir Brian Pitman published an article about his career. It mentioned that in 1992 Lloyds Bank lodged a hostile takeover of Midland Bank. The deal ended in defeat for the Bank as it claimed the price was too high. Sir Brian Pearse, the former CEO of Midland Bank recalled that, during negotiations, Pitman was asked what he intended to call the new bank. He suggested sticking with the Lloyds Bank name. 'That way, we only have to change half of the signs,' he said to raised eyebrows, before adding and 'half of the stationery'.

August 2002 saw the start of Aylesbury branch refurbishment. Unfortunately there was so much rubbish that the skip overflowed. Staff were called out in the early hours of the morning as a small fire had started. Passers-by were seen to remove some of the furniture and cars were brought in to take it away. Enough was left the following day for Roger Lord, Catherine Letton and Jonathan Griffiths to demonstrate the mess the workmen had made.

Chairmen since 1977

1977 Sir Jeremy Morse

1993 Sir Robin Ibbs

1997 Sir Brian Pitman

2001 Maarten Van den Bergh

2006 Sir Victor Blank

2009 Sir Winfried Bischoff

2014 Lord Blackwell

Lord (Norman) Blackwell, a former business consultant who also worked as an adviser to John Major and Margaret Thatcher, succeeded Sir Winfried Bischoff as Chairman of Lloyds Banking Group on 3 April 2014.

25 Gresham Street is the head office of Lloyds Bank. The 120,000 sq ft building was completed in 2002. It provides 10 floors of column free office space. The site straddles the remains of a roman fort. The south facing atrium is flanked by two office wings suspended over a column-free entrance hall. The adjacent garden was originally the St John Zachary Churchyard.

Roll of Honour

This memorial book records the names of the Directorate and Staff of the Lloyds TSB Group who have lost their lives during times of war. The book is kept inside the entrance lobby at Gresham Street head office.

The memorial that stands outside the Gresham Street head office. It reads 'In remembrance of all employees of the Lloyds TSB Group who have given their lives in times of conflict'. A war memorial graced the entrance lobby in the former head office in Lombard Street for 83 years until it was moved in 2004 to the retail banking headquarters at Canons House in Bristol. The names of 686 men who were killed in action or died of their wounds are inscribed on a black marble tablet.

Below is a list of the 686 men listed on the Lloyds Bank war memorial in Bristol who lost their lives in the First World War. They include individuals who worked for two banks taken over by Lloyds at the very end of the war (1918–1919), namely Capital and Counties and the West Yorkshire Bank. These details have been collated by the Bank from the memorial and the memorial album.

A
Ablitt, Albert H
Adams, Edwin J
Adams, Thomas
Aldrich, George R
Allen, Edward A F
Allen, Mervyn R W
Allport, Allan H
Almond, James E
Ancell, Horace
Andrews, Alfred A
Anstey, Thomas E J
Arnold, Ernest F
Arnott, Frederick
Astle, Reginald W
Atha, Leonard E
B
Back, Erroll W A
Bailey, Robert C
Baker, Frank V
Bakewell, George J
Baldwin, John E
Balls, Frank W
Bannister, Henry W
Bardwell, Frank G W
Barker, Edgar B
Barker, Percy D D
Barnes, Herbert J
Barnes, Wilfred O
Barnett, William A
Barnett, William R
Barr, David W
Bastard, Charles S
Batchelar, Robert T
Bath, Harold F
Battye, John
Bayley, Reginald J,
Beacall, Arthur
Beak, Douglas E
Beare, Robert V
Bell, Charles D
Bell, Howard D
Benbow, John L
Bennett, Ralph
Bennett, Sidney F
Bentley, Frederick
Bestow, Leslie W
Bettison, Mark H
Bevan, Hedley
Bird, Ernest W
Bishop, Frank E
Bloomer, Arnold G
Boaden, Harold J
Boardley, Harold
Bolton, Percy J
Bond, Charles E
Borer, Frederick W V

Bothamley, Richard A,
Boucher, Frederick H
Boughton, Robert H
Breyen, Francis
Bridgman, William L
Brinkworth, Edwin J
Brodbeck, Edwin C
Bromham, Charles A R
Brouard, Ernest J
Brown, Edward D
Brown, Edwin P W
Brown, Norman A
Browning, George H
Bryant, Richard L A
Bull, Henry M
Bullen, George B
Bunce, John F
Burch, Edward G
Bye, Cecil F
Byrt, Douglas R
C
Caines, John A H
Calvert, Eric R
Cann, Leonard E
Carlisle, Francis B
Carr, Alexander G
Carsberg, Albert
Carter, Francis R G
Carter, John T
Carter, Ronald J F
Carty, William G
Cates, Geoffrey
Celaschi, Robert P J
Chapman, Joseph
Charlton, Norman E
Charlton, William G
Chew, Norman G
Christie, James A
Clarke, Gerald F
Clarke, Samuel F
Clarke, Stanley V
Cleaver, Sydney C
Clegg, Cyril T
Clinch, James H
Cochrane, Reginald
Cockburn, George P
Cockburn, Sidney
Cohen, Wilfred J
Cole, Henry M
Cole, Sidney L F
Cole, William T
Cook, Henry C
Cooke, William H C
Cooper, Arthur C
Cooper, Francis Y
Cooper, Wilfrid O,
Corbridge, Arthur

Cordiner, Theodore G
Cortis, John H
Coster, Keith H
Couldridge, Jack O
Cowin, Henry H
Cowley, Frederick John
Cox, Cyril H
Cox, Richard
Creedy, Edmund E
Crisp, Ernest G
Croft, John E
Crosby, John C P,
Crouch, Alan
Crowther, Guy
Crowther, Jack
Crowther, John
Cullum, Clement J B
Cuss, Cyril
D
Dain, John L
Dames, Charles L
Daniel, Edwin C
Daniel, Evan T
Davenport, Edgell
Davey, Charles L
Davey, Ronald T
Davies, Arthur R
Davies, Benjamin D R
Davies, David F
Davies, David H
Davies, David R
Davies, David
Davies, John
Davies, John P
Davies, Morgan R
Davis, Charles G
Davis, Horace J
Davison, Frederick
Dawson, Dan M
Day, Gerald H
Day, Harry M
De Lattre, Reginald
Dealey, Louis J B
Dean, Reginald C
Decent, William E
Denham, Eric M
Denison, Robert C
Denny, Guy
Derry, Daniel
Dicken, Geoffrey
Dicks, Francis J N
Dickson, Ronald A C
Dinnis, George H
Down, Robert H
Downer, Frederick
Downes, Donald L
Drake, Percy A

Drinkwater, Leonard W
Duckworth, Percy B
Dulley, David C C
Duly, Percy W,
Duncan, Kenneth W A
Durston, Montague G T
Dyer, John M
E
Eagar, Francis H
Early, Cecil D,
Early, Egbert E
Easlea, Algernon H P
Ecclestone, Ebor
Edwards, Britton J
Elkins, Benjamin D
Ellen, Harry J
Ellis, Charles J
Ellis, Robert T H
Ellison, Sydney W
Elly, Cyril J,
Elsmere, Llewllyn B
Errington, James
Evans, Alfred D
Evans, David G
Evans, John B
Evans, John T
Evans, Thomas J
Evans-Davies, Thomas A J
Everson, Charles P
Ewer, Harold T
F
Fellows, Harold J
Ferris, Francis W
Few, Robert J D
Field, Roger G
Finch, Claude F
Flux, Leonard G
Franklin, Hollister C
Fraser, Laurence R
Frazer, Douglas V
Freeman, Charles
Frith, Charles V
Furse, William H
G
Gallichan, Raymond J
Gamble, Harry N
Garrett, William R
George, Frank W
George, Stanley
Gibbs, Harold W
Gilbert, Joseph P
Gilkes, Norman S
Glanvile, William S
Goodrich, John E
Goodwyn, Arthur W
Goulding, John C
Gramshaw, Eric

Grant, Stanley K
Grantham, Edward
Gratwick, Harold D
Green, Charles H
Green, Leonard J
Greenham, Donald W
Greenwood, Joseph H
Gregory, Arthur W
Griffin, Stanley R
Griffiths, Arthur H
Griffiths, Thomas
Grist, Ronald
Gudge, Rodney C
Guest, Percival J
Gummer, Basil A

H

Hadley, Edgar W
Haines, Stephen G
Haldane, Donald
Hallpike, Christopher G
Hambly, Alan
Hambly, Cyril,
Hambly, Dudley C
Hamilton, William W
Hammond, Kenneth L C
Hammond, William C
Hands, Leslie H
Hardcastle, Frederick W
Harding, Charles H
Harding, Cyril G
Hards, Cyril R
Hardy, Phillip E R
Harper, Francis B
Harper, James,
Harries, Albert G H
Harris, Charles H
Harris, Harold M
Harris, Henry J R
Harris, John G R
Harris, William F
Harvey, John
Hatton, Christopher
Hawken, George B
Hawkes, Percival W
Haydon, Gilbert,
Hayes, Richard J
Hayman, Hubert F
Heath, Bryan
Hemming, Edward G
Hemming, Stanley
Henderson, Jacob J
Hensman, Henry J
Henson, Albert T H
Heppell, Thomas R
Hewitt, Humphrey
Hibbs, Richard J W
Hickman, Ernest J
Hicks-Beach, Michael
Hugh (see also Quenington, Viscount)
Higgs, Albert
High, Gilbert C
Higham, Edward D
Hill, Alec L,

Hill, Charles L
Hillier, Sidney N
Hills, Lawrence C
Hind, Reginald J
Hinds, Thomas P
Hipkiss, Albert V
Hitchens, Stuart R
Hocking, Leonard V
Hodgson, Harold A
Hodgson, John F
Holland, Wilfred
Holt, John W
Hooper, Henry E
Hore, Cecil W
Horne, George C
Hornsby, Rowland H
Hoult, Powis A
Howard, Sidney I
Hudson, George T
Hughes, John O
Hullett, Lionel J
Humphries, Leslie G
Hunt, Sydney E
Hybart, John

I

Ikin, Herbert L
Illingworth, Charles C
Ingleton, Hubert J
Innes, John
Inwood, Walter S
Isaac, Arthur W
Ison, Charles F
Ivatts, Selwyn

J

James, Clarence E
Jeffrey, Reginald H
Jenkins, Joseph C W
Jenkins, Trevor K
Jennings, Frederick
Jennings, Walter
Jennings, William J
Jessup, William H G
Johnson, Evelyn W J
Jones, Basil R
Jones, David T
Jones, Hugh L
Jones, Ithel
Jones, John C
Jones, Owen A
Jones, Robert C
Jones, Russell H
Jones, Stanley N
Jones, Wilfred E
Jopling, Albert E
Julian, Edgar J

K

Keenlyside, Thomas E
Keevil, Albert F M
Keevil, John F
Kelly, Gilbert H
Kent, George E
Kernick, Thomas R
King, Robert D
King, William E

Kingsland, John W
Kingsman, Ronald W
Kitson, George B
Kitts, John F E
Knaggs, Henry H
Knapp, Edward M
Knowler, William J A

L

Lampard, Percy
Lampey, William E,
Langford, Arthur H A
Langrish, Thomas H
Launder, Henry N
Laverton, Frederick K
Le Brun, Lewis A
Ledeboer, Douglas H
Le Gros, Claude D
Leale, Frederick R
Leigh-Bennett, Olliph S
Lewis, Albert
Lewis, Arthur J
Lewis, George A D
Lewis, Harold L
Lewis, Thomas G
Lindley, Leonard F
Littleford, Harold A
Lloyd, Trevor M
Loader, Graham C
Lockstone, Edward S
Lockyer, Felix C
Lofts, Wilfred
Looker, Geoffrey V R
Lott, William
Lowther, George A
Loye, Reginald P
Lyte, Owen N

M

Malcolm, Stuart R
Marsh, Nicholas C
Marshall, Arthur N
Marshall, Dudley
Marshall, William D
Martin, Reginald F
Martin, Walter
Matthews, John E N
Mauger, George E
Mauger, Gerald
May, Walter G
Maybrey, Arthur J
McDonnell, Thomas J
McFadyean, Ronald
McKee, John A
McLare, Alexander V
McMichael, Colin J W
Meade, Wakefield W
Meakin, Sidney A
Melrose, Thomas N
Mercer, Alex W G
Mercer, George E
Meredith, Malcolm H
Merry, Philip S
Mewett, Walter
Meynell, Hugo C J
Michael, Richard G

Middleton, John
Miles, Gordon
Millard, Harold G M
Millard, Stewart R
Milledge, Sidney J
Minett, William V
Misselbrook, Alfred W
Mitchell, Colin
Mitchell, Francis F
Mitchell, Lawrence A
Moir, Douglas D D K
Mondy, Neville C
Moorhouse, Sidney E
Morgan, Cecil H L
Morgan, Richard G
Morgan, William I
Morris, Charles R M
Morris, Emrys
Mortimer, Reginald
Morton, Arthur D
Mott, Alfred L
Murch, James H

N

Nash, Ronald M
Nattress, William
Neeves, Ivor S
Nicholls, Harold J
North, Robert D
Norton, Eric
Nutt, Percy J

O

O'Halloran, Sylvester N E
Olden, Sidney M
Oram, John M
Osborne, Francis R
O'Shea, Dermot T
Osman, Clifford S
Ostler, Thomas,
Owen, Thomas S

P

Page, Clive A
Page, Edward C
Page, Thomas S
Paige, Jack B
Painter, Henry S
Palk, Leonard
Palmer, Edward C M
Parsell, John E
Paterson, Allan F
Pattinson, Robert B
Paull, Walter R
Payne, Charles H
Payne, Hedley S
Peal, Archibald T
Pearce, Joseph John
Pearson, William G
Pedersen, Cecil P G
Peel, Roger E
Penson, Arthur R
Penson, Lionel R
Pepperday, Gerald A G
Perkins, George W
Perrott, William T
Perry, Henry B

Phillips, Charles E
Phillips, Leonard H P
Phillips, Richard M
Phipps, Arthur G
Phipps, Charles P
Pickard, Ernest W
Pittham, Frederick T
Ponting, Geoffrey
Popplestone, Archibald H
Poston, Charles H
Potter, Augustine T
Potter, Keith E
Potts, Lewis M
Powe, Percy
Powell, John A
Powell, Philip G W A A
Prangley, Norman C
Pratt, Lionel H
Preston, George G
Price, Horace C
Price, Wilfred
Priestley, Douglas B
Primrose, Hugh R
Proffitt, John T R
Pryor, Edgar H
Pullin, Ernest A
Pym, Norman H

Q

Quenington, Viscount, director (see also Hicks-Beach, Michael Hugh)

R

Radford, Joseph
Rainsbury, Frederick T,
Randall, Harold V
Ratcliffe-Gaylard, Eric R
Ravenhill, Harold H
Rawlins, Roy D
Rawlinson, Harry R
Read, Edward M
Reaney, Harold A
Redding, Thomas
Reddrop, Reginald T
Rex, Harold W
Reynish, Horace J C
Richards, Ewart W
Richards, Harold G
Richards, Percival M,
Ridding, Laurance J F R
Ridley, Thomas
Rigby, Harry F
Roberts, Emrys J
Roberts, John H
Roberts, Morris
Robertson, George C
Robinson, Walter J
Roe, William H B
Rogers, Francis J,
Rogers, Stanley
Rolph, Joseph C J
Rose, Reginald V
Rosher, Max L
Rowe, Simeon,

Rowswell, Herbert
Rudledge, Thomas W
Ruegg, Maurice C
Rundell, Gerald E
Rundle, Edwin J
Rundle, Sydney H
Russell, George W H

S

Sadler, Frank
Sainsbury, Charles
Salter, Alfred R
Salway, Douglas J
Sampson, Leslie L
Sanders, Cecil C
Sanders, Stephen A F
Sanderson, Ronald
Sargeant, Ralph L
Saunders, Robert
Scott, Kenneth T
Secker, Frank T
Sedgley, Henry F
Sedgwick, Harold
Seline, Joseph J
Severs, John
Seymour, Herbert A
Sharp, Eric, Dover
Sharpley, John T
Shaw, Robert R S
Shea, Arthur H
Shepard, Bernard A
Sherrard, Bertram
Shinner, Bernard
Short, Cyril S T
Siddall, Thomas A
Skyrme, Richard E E
Slade, John H B
Slater, Frederic
Smart, Eric D
Smith, Charles E
Smith, Jack
Smith, Norman L
Smith, Percy
Smith, Philip S
Smith, Stephen H
Smitten, George A
Spargo, Loris S
Spencer, Thomas K
Squires, Wilfred S
Stallard, James A
Stannard, Geoffrey M
Starkey, Joseph B C
Starling, Clarence R
Steer, Henry D G
Stephens, John S
Stevens, Alfred J
Stevenson, Colin
Stockman, William E
Stocks, William H
Stone, Edward A F
Stones, Shepherd
Stott, Edward B
Stubbs, William E
Stubbs, William N
Stuckey, Ralph H

Sutton, Gurney S
Swayne, Arthur D C
Symons, Thomas S

T

Talbot, Edgar F
Tanner, Montague A
Tarrant, Albert H C
Tate, Edward
Tattersall, Philip C P
Taylor, Charles E
Taylor, Guy C V
Taylor, John B
Taylor, Leonard B
Taylor, Robert L
Theobald, Edgar M
Thew, William R
Thomas, Arthur B T
Thomas, Arthur C
Thomas, Daniel G
Thomas, David A
Thomas, David J
Thomas, Percy K
Thomas, Reginald I V C
Thomas, Victor G A
Thomas, William E
Thompson, Eric,
Thuell, William J
Thwaites, Harry H
Titjen, Carsten F H
Titmuss, Frederick
Todd, Charles H
Tozer, Stanley M
Trew, Edwin C
Triphook, Owen L
Truman, Thomas A
Tucker, Ralph C
Tudor, Hubert J
Turnbull, Andrew N
Turner, James
Twine, William H
Twining, Cecil F H

U

Upfield, Nelson
Urry, Frank A

V

Varey, John A
Vicary, William D
Vickers, Frank J
Voller, Sydney G

W

Wagstaff, Robert A
Wakefield, Linton F
Walker, Herbert
Walker, Joseph A
Ward, Edward J
Ward, Ewart W D
Warren, Reginald D
Waterhouse, Arthur H
Waugh, William
Weeks, Reginald S
Welch, Robert M
Welchman, Patrick E
Westlake, George
Whidborne, Charles H

White, Reginald S
White, William D F
White, William E C
Whitehouse, Frank
Wicking, Wilfred R
Wilbee, Reginald F
Wilkinson, Bertram M
Wilkinson, Frank
Wilkinson, Frederick J
Willcock, Cecil B
Williams, Douglas J S
Williams, Eric V O
Williams, John
Williams, John R
Williams, Thomas E
Williams, Trevor L
Williams, Vivian P
Wilshin, John H
Wilson, Alexander D
Wilson, James A
Wilson, William S
Wise, Henry L
Wiseman, Bruce
Wolton, Owen B
Wood, George G B
Wood, John
Woodcock, Frederick A
Woodward, Thomas C
Wooster, Gerald H
Wooster, Horace E
Wootton, Hubert T
Worthington, Arthur,
Wright, Harold
Wright, Robert A
Wyborn, William
Wylde, Charles G A

Y

Yardley, Alan
Yeatman, John F
Young, William L

Important Dates and Events

1992 The Bank tried and failed to take over the old Midland bank.

1995 Acquired one of Britain's biggest building societies the Cheltenham & Gloucester Building Society. This was the first ever association between a bank and a building society.

1995 Merged with TSB to form Lloyds TSB. It was to be another four years before the bank became a High Street name. The bank traded as Lloyds TSB Bank plc between 1999 and 2013.

2000 Lloyds TSB completed the purchase of Scottish Widows. With this acquisition, the Bank inherited one of the strongest brands in the insurance industry.

2001 Attempt to take over the Abbey National, which was blocked by the competition commission who ruled that a merger would be against the public interest.

2006 Lack of compliance surrounding PPI (payment protection insurance) resulted in the bank and other major PPI providers being fined for not treating customers fairly. In 2012 Lloyds announced that that they had set aside £3.6 billion to cover the cost of compensating customers who were mis-sold PPI.

2009 January. In the midst of a global financial crisis, Lloyds TSB took over HBOS plc. The new company instantly became the largest retail bank in the UK. Lloyds Banking Group now served more than 25 million customers, and brought together a host of well-known brands. These included Bank of Scotland, Birmingham Midshires, Cheltenham & Gloucester, Halifax, Lloyds TSB, and Scottish Widows.

2012 Lloyds TSB was the Official Banking and Insurance Partner of the London 2012 Olympic and Paralympic Games.

2009 Government take 43.4% stake as part of UK bank rescue package.

2013 Lloyds TSB renamed Lloyds Bank. The familiar black horse logo was given a make-over for the relaunch of Lloyds Bank on the high street. And more than 630 branches were brought together across Britain to form the new TSB.

2013 Fined £28m for 'serious failings' in relation to the bonus scheme for sales staff. The FCA said that he bonus scheme pressurised staff to hit sales targeted or risk being demoted and have their pay cut.

2015 A milestone year for Lloyds Banking Group. It is the 200th anniversary of Scottish Widows, the 250th anniversary of Lloyds Bank and the 30th year of the Lloyds Bank Foundations.

2015 Dividend resumed. The Bank, which has one of the UK's largest shareholder bases, was historically one of the most generous dividend payers in the FTSE 100, but had not been able to pay out since the financial crisis struck as it attempted to rebuild itself. It last announced an interim payment in August 2008 to its 3m shareholders just weeks before its £20bn bailout.

Family Tree

The family tree shows just a few of the most significant takeovers.

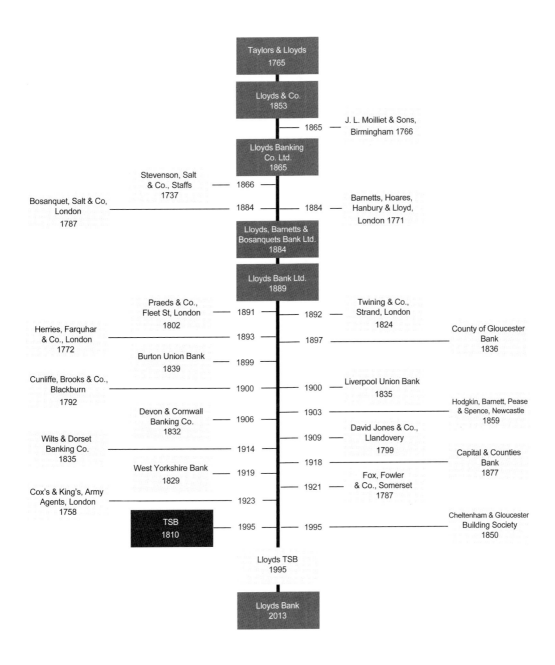

Bibliography

In researching this publication the author has drawn a great deal from the written work of other writers and publications:

Bank of London and South America: A Short History 1862-1970, published by Economics Intelligence Dept, BOLSA, 40-66 Queen Victoria Street, 1970.

Banking World.

British Banks and Banking: A Pictorial History, R.M. Fitzmaurice, D. Bradford Barton Ltd.

Debtors to their Profession (A History of the Institute of Bankers 1879-1979), Edwin Green, Metheun and Co Ltd, 1979.

International Banking, Robert McKee, Wayland Publishers Ltd, 1981.

Lloyds Bank, Robert McKee, Wayland Publishers Ltd, 1982.

Lloyds Bank 1918-1969, J.R. Winton, Oxford University Press, 1982.

Lloyds Bank in the History of English Banking, R. S. Sayers, Oxford University Press, 1957.

Lloyds Bank Group website

Lloyds Bank News

The Dark Horse

The Staff Magazine

The Story of the Banks, J. F. Ashby, Hutchinson and Co Ltd. 1934.

The Story of Lloyds Bank, booklet published by Lloyds Bank, 1977.

Index